THERAPY
and how to avoid it!
A guide for the perplexed

ALSO BY NIGEL PLANER

I, an actor
A Good Enough Dad
Let's Get Divorced
Neil's Book of the Dead

ALSO BY ROBERT LLEWELLYN

The Reconstructed Heart
The Man in the Rubber Mask
Thin He Was and Filthy Haired

Nigel Planer & Robert Llewellyn

Therapy
and how to avoid it!
A guide for the perplexed

Hodder & Stoughton

For Lionel Kreeger, one of the good guys.

Checked for psychic hygiene by Roberta Green, Assoc.
APP, Memb I.G.A.
C***-word courtesy of John Dowie.

First published in 1996 by Hodder and Stoughton
A division of Hodder Headline PLC.

10 9 8 7 6 5 4 3 2 1

A CIP catalogue record for this title is available
from the British Library.

ISBN 0 340 64905 4

Typeset by Palimpsest Book Production Limited,
Polmont, Stirlingshire
Printed and bound in Great Britain by
Mackays of Chatham PLC, Chatham, Kent

Hodder and Stoughton
A division of Hodder Headline PLC
338 Euston Road
London NW1 3BH

We are poor indeed if we are only sane.

D. W. Winnicott

CONTENTS

1

THE CALL

A phone rings. A man's voice groans loudly and curses. The phone continues to ring. There is no movement, then suddenly the bed covers are thrown back in a flurry of angry activity.

Nigel   Aaargh. Forgot to put the answerphone on!

Nigel picks up the phone and has trouble with the cable – it's wrapped around the base unit. More curses as finally he holds the phone next to his ear.

Nigel   Yes?

There is a sound of swallowing on the other end.

Nigel   Hello?

Nigel is just about to put the phone back down when he hears a hoarse whisper.

Robert It's me, man. I'm dying. I'm dying, I'm that close to the edge man . . . It's crazy in here. My head is full of . . . conundrums. I'm dangling. (*He laughs*) God, I must sound mental. D'you think I sound mental?

Nigel   Hello. Who is this?

Robert It's me.

1

Nigel   Who am I talking to?

Robert   Nige. Nige. Nige. Nige. It's Robert.

Nigel   Who?

Robert   Robert. Robert Llewellyn. Robert Llewellyn. Robert Llewellyn. Exactly! Who is he? I mean, who am I, really? You know.

Nigel   How'd you get my number?

Robert   Look, I'm really sorry about this, but I don't know who else to call. My fingers just went on the buttons, they just went on the buttons.

Nigel   It's okay. Take your time.

There is a long silence.

Robert   Are you still there, Nige?

Nigel   I'm here.

Robert   Ah, what a relief. I'm sorry about this. I'm a bit calmer now. I really needed to speak to someone you know.

Nigel   Who gave you my number? This number's unlisted.

Robert   You gave it to me.

Nigel   Did I? When?

Robert Couple of years ago, at that benefit we did together, at the London Palladium. The *Hysteria* thing, Terrence Higgins Trust. My bit was cut from the telly version.

Nigel What?

Robert I don't know why, it was a sketch with Tony Slattery and Craig Ferguson. It went down okay, but they cut it.

Nigel Are you ringing to tell me that?

Robert No, I need, you know, some help. Well, a bit of advice actually.

Nigel What time is it?

Robert Well I waited until after six.

Nigel So how long after six is it?

Robert About three minutes. I've been awake all night and I thought you might be the only person who understands what I'm going through. You see, at the party after the charity gig you kept saying how similar we were. You know, because we've both played the down-trodden guy in a sit-com and we know how that does your head in, and you said it felt like some sort of common bond.

Nigel Did I?

Robert That's what you said at the party when you kept hugging me.

Nigel Did I hug you?

Robert You said we must both have a similar unresolved oedipal transferential dysfunction, don't you remember? Blew my mind. 'Cos we both had to hide behind masks before we could say what we really felt, and it was really our way of expressing our hostility to the outside world. 'Cos the only way people like you and me could be successful was by pretending to be failures.

Nigel I said all that?

Robert Yeah, and then you fell over.

Nigel Why are you telling me this?

Robert Well, you've been in therapy, haven't you?

Nigel Who told you that?

Robert Well, you seemed to know so much about it. You were talking about it for hours.

Nigel I was obviously very drunk. But there's a big difference between talking about it and actually doing it . . .

Robert Yes, you're right, I shouldn't have rung you. Just clutching at straws, you know how it is.

Nigel . . . although sometimes those without firsthand experience can have an empirical overview which throws more light on a subject than those who are too involved to see what's really going on. So what's the problem, Robert?

Robert Well, Danielle's left me, but it's not that. I mean I can understand why she'd leave me. Any woman in their right mind would leave me. I think it goes deeper than that. I think it's to do with not really knowing who my real self is. I think something really deep inside is fundamentally flawed.

Nigel   I see, and how long have you felt like this?

Robert   Well, not long.

Nigel   And before that, nothing?

Robert   Oh, I see. Well, no, always I suppose. I've never really been me. The other week, I just looked in the mirror for hours, without blinking, and in the end, my reflection said, 'What you looking at, Jimmy?' I mean, Jimmy! He didn't even know my name.

Nigel   And you feel some kind of treatment might help you to make friends with yourself?

Robert   Well, that's what I'm asking about. I think I might need to go, only I'm not sure, and I was thinking of going today to see some therapist or other, but how do I know it's the right sort? I'm worried I might open doors which are best left shut. You know, go really doolally. Like tonight.

Nigel   Yes, there's always that worry.

Robert   I'm not sure if I really should go. Or if I really need to.

Nigel   I should think you probably need to do something.

Robert You think so? Yes. Right, well that's why I rang, I was wondering if I could maybe have a chat with you. You know, to see how you felt about this.

Nigel I see.

Robert Look. I'm nearly forty, I'm alive, I should be happy. The reason I'm not happy is deep and complex and requires analysis. Are you busy?

Nigel I think I've got a voice over from ten to eleven.

Robert Fantastic. Where?

Nigel Silk Sound. Berwick Street.

Robert I'll meet you there at eleven, then.

Nigel Well, okay, I mean I may have a lunch meeting or something, you know.

Robert Sure. No problem. Brilliant. Thanks, Nige. I really need this. You know, it's all become a little ... you know. I'm really indebted to you. Did I wake you up?

Nigel No, no. I was more or less awake anyway.

Robert Okay. See you at eleven, then.

Nigel drops the phone in its cradle and flops back onto his pillow.

ROBERT'S DIARY
JUNE 14TH 6.15 am

Just rang Nigel Planer. Think I may have woken him which is a total nightmare, but he seems really nice. Bit arrogant, but at the moment that's fine with me. I'm so lost I need someone arrogant to show me the way. After not being able to get any sleep for weeks, listening to Nigel has made me really hopeful.

Finally doing something about it has made me excited. I think this is going to be a turning point, I've let things get way out of whack for months, but for the first time this morning, I could almost feel my hands on the controls again. I could pull this sucker out of a nosedive if I could just remember how to fly. Wow, that's a good analogy, I'll tell Nigel that one when I see him today. Life as a plane in a nosedive with a dead pilot, and the blood's spurting out of his neck all over the windows, and I can't see out, Oh God, and the girl behind me is screaming, sweat pouring down her long brown neck, and her shirt is sticking to her skin . . .

NIGEL'S Diary
JUNE 14TH 9.20 am

Oh God, Robert Llewellyn. What do I do now? At least he seems to have forgotten the time he stood on my doorstep for ten hours with a can of Special Brew in his cold blistered hand trying to bum a tenner off me. I've heard he doesn't wreck bars any more, but you never know. We all feel sorry for Robert, but cross the road to avoid him in case he brings out that fluffy old clip about his last one-man show.

He's such a loose cannon, he rings me at six in the bloody morning to ask me if I think he needs therapy! I must admit though, of all people, it has to be said he probably came to the right place. Unless he was winding me up, another Llewellyn scam. He's so desperate, scrabbling around for a new idea, he'd try anything. But there was a certain tone in his voice which told me he might just be, dare I say it, genuine. And I might be able to help. But would he listen?

What am I saying? The thought of a neat and tidy Robert Llewellyn talking about 'dysfunctional relationships' with Joan Bakewell on Heart of the Matter is just too grim, he's probably better off like he is. I suppose I'll have to buy him a meal and send him on his way, poor bastard.

2

DO YOU REALLY WANT TO LIFT THE LID?

*Robert Llewellyn and Nigel Planer enter a West End café at
11.30 in the morning. A few customers are scattered through
the dense cluster of tables, the kitchen staff are busy preparing
for the lunchtime rush. Robert and Nigel stand in the centre of
the café in what appears to be a state of indecision.*

Nigel   Look Robert, we're not that similar. We're just
two guys with fairly similar experiences who work in
TV comedy series and play characters which necessitate
some fairly self-negating disguise. Neil, with his long hippy
wig and flares, and Kryten, a character with no penis who
dresses in rubber.

Robert   Hang on, hang on. When you say no penis, you
have to remember Kryten is not human, he is android

robotic, mechanoid to be precise, and would not be expected to have a penis, as such.

Nigel   Oh, yeah. Alright.

Robert   He has got a groinal socket.

Nigel   Oh, really.

Robert   With numerous add-on fittings.

Nigel   Sure, sure. Understood.

Robert and Nigel stand awkwardly for a moment.

Robert   Anyway, I thought we were supposed to be talking about therapy and me. That's what I need to talk about. I don't know anything about your personal life and all, but you've always struck me as being really sorted out. You're sort of emotionally balanced, aren't you? You're centred, you're together, you're whole. I want to be like you, man. I want that, but I don't know where to start. I looked in the ads in the back of *Time Out*. The help section, I mean, not the lonely hearts, although I did have a recurring problem with that once. No, I mean the therapy and growth section, and you know what, it was a total maze. There were nude gestalt drumming therapists and loving awareness weekends in a castle in Sussex.

Nigel   It *is* a maze. But what's interesting is that anyone medically qualified is not allowed to advertise. So, any therapist who advertises is by default medically untrained. This doesn't necessarily mean they're no good or corrupt, just that they won't have had straight clinical experience.

Robert I never thought of that.

Nigel It can be very confusing.

They fall into silence again. Robert looks around the room as Nigel scuffs his shoe across a stain on the floor.

Robert This place is brilliant, I've never been here before. Do they do vegetarian?

Nigel Of course. I never would have thought you were a veggie.

Robert I'm not, but maybe I ought to become one. Maybe I've already got BSE, which might be the problem.

Nigel Robert, you're not a cow, you can't actually get BSE. You could possibly catch CJD, which is the human form of the disease.

Robert Where are the toilets?

Nigel Just down those stairs, they're not too bad.

Nigel follows Robert who sits down at a table in the centre of the café.

Nigel You don't want to go now, then?

Robert No, I just like to know where they are.

Nigel   Is this table alright for you, Robert?

Robert   Yeah, it's fine.

Nigel   What about that one over there?

Nigel points to a table in the corner of the restaurant.

Robert   Yes. Sure, whatever.

They move and Robert sits down at a table by the wall. Nigel stands awkwardly.

Nigel   I've learnt there's no point denying the fact that I can't eat when I'm boxed in. I don't want to sit in the corner, so do you mind going in that seat? Sorry.

Robert   No, no, of course not. Help yourself.

Robert moves into the corner seat by the wall.

Robert   Do you think I need therapy?

Nigel   Well, you do seem pretty jumpy to me.

Robert   It's still a bloody difficult decision. You know, to take that first step. I'm scared I'd lose all my creative skills if I sorted myself out. I mean, look at Buster Keaton.[1] As a kid he was part of his parents' vaudeville act; slapstick routines, he was hit and smashed and beaten on a daily basis, they really whacked him, bruises and stuff. They told him not to show anything on his face, just take the blows. I mean, talk about abuse. The question is, would his films have been so good without that? If he'd been through a huge amount of therapy, he may have been happier, but would he still've been able to do what he did? Doesn't genius come out of pain?[2]

Nigel   So you think you may be a genius, Robert? You know, Freud actually said analysis is not going to solve all your problems, the best it can do is replace neurotic misery with ordinary unhappiness.[3] Look at me, we're talking about Freud already and it's only 11.30.

Robert   But do I want my problem solved? Because what will it be like being better, will it change who I am? How am I going to function without my problem? This is my problem, sitting here, it's me. It may be bad, but it's mine.

Nigel   Yes, I understand. It can be difficult to let go of a problem, can't it? Apart from anything else, you're getting quite a lot out of it in the way of attention and sympathy. And of course you can use it as an excuse to avoid meeting your responsibilities, or simply to justify your failures to yourself . . .

Robert fingers the menu nervously.

Nigel   . . . that's what's meant by secondary gain.

Robert   Secondary gain. Oh God. I'd have to learn a whole new load of terms, wouldn't I?

Nigel   Not really, Robert. Only if you choose to.

13

Robert Hang on, if that's a secondary gain, what's the primary gain?

Nigel Well, obviously, that you can avoid facing up to what's actually wrong, which allows you to continue pretending to be happy. Remember that old saying, there's three things you can do to get attention as a kid? Be brilliant, be difficult, or be ill. Which one are you, Robert?

Robert Oh God. I've never even thought about this stuff. You're so sorted out.

Nigel Well, yes, I suppose I *am* sorted out now. It's not been easy, I'm very English that way, I tend to bottle things up, but when I go, it can get rather unpleasant. I was always having tantrums as a child. Well, until quite recently, actually. Well I haven't had one for . . . a few months now. Weeks.

Robert I suppose, um, well I was almost a genius, not quite but almost. Not much trouble, and rarely ill. I did a quite good puppet show when I was about nine. Not that good, my mum and dad got up and left halfway through. But it can't be that. What's happening to me now is the worst thing I've ever had to deal with. Sometimes I stay up all night scratching. I know there's nothing wrong, medically, so it must all be psychosomatic.

Nigel Aha!

Robert What? You don't think it's psychosomatic? Maybe I'm dying of some weird skin disorder.

Nigel   No, no, it's just that so many people have the wrong idea about psychosomatic illness. They think it means some sort of invented physical symptom which has been actually brought on by the mind and is therefore in some way not real. And the next thing you know you're being accused of being a hypochondriac. It's ridiculous.

Robert   What, have you been accused of that, then?

Nigel   It used to happen all the time, but I've learnt how to cherish myself. No, if there's a link between the power of the mind and physical illness, it must be subconscious. That's the point. Psychosomatic doesn't mean the mind causing illness, or conjuring up illness. It's a two-way thing, the mind and the body working symbiotically, irretrievably linked together. 'Psycho-' the mind, 'soma-' the body.

Robert   Is that what it means?

Nigel   Yes. The mind and body working in conjunction to make you the fucked-up, rash-ridden half-person you think you are. When people use the word psychosomatic these days, what they really mean is psychogenic. Now that *does* mean a physical symptom that is caused by the mind.

Robert   Hey, you look great when you're angry. If only casting directors could see you like this, you could be in *Prime Suspect* or something.

Nigel   That's very kind of you, Robert, but it's your internalised anger we're here to discuss.

Robert. Oh, yeah. Sorry.

A young waitress approaches them carrying a menu.

Nigel Hello, Kelly. I'll have the special.

Kelly The special. Alright, Mr Planer. You alright?

Nigel I'm fine, thank you, Kelly. This is Robert.

Kelly Is he your brother?

Nigel Good heavens, no.

Robert Wow, spooky. We *are* the same.

Kelly What would you like, sir?

Robert I'll have a ham salad. No, a tuna salad. No, I'll have the ham. The ham. No, I'll have the cheese.

Nigel Have the cheese.

Robert Yeah, I'll have the cheese.

Nigel He'll have the cheese, Kelly. Please. And two teas.

Robert Could I change mine?

Kelly You don't want the cheese salad?

Robert Well, no. If that's alright. I'd like to change it to the special.

Kelly   You want the special.

Robert   Yes, please.

Kelly   That's two specials, then.

Kelly walks away, scratching her pen across the order pad quite violently.

Robert   I've got to be careful with cheese. I always forget.

Nigel   Are you lactoallergic?

Robert   No, I don't think so, I just worry that it makes me smell funny. I don't want women to think I smell cheesy. What's the special?

Nigel   Vegetarian thali.

Robert   Thank God for that. Has it got cheese in it?

Nigel   No. No dairy products.

Robert   Oh, thank God.

Nigel   Allergies are complex little buggers, aren't they? You never know if you've got one. I worried for years that I might have one and not know about it. I went to an allergist once. I took batteries of tests, my forearm was a mass of blistered skin. She tried me with every known irritant, rash-inducing herbs, mites that live under your skin, microbugs that live in your lower gut and bowel.

I was allergic to everything. There was a time when it looked like I would have to live in an oxygen tent on a drip for the rest of my life, except I thought I might be allergic to stainless steel so I couldn't have a needle in my arm. But then I couldn't follow it through because I got a load of work offers and forgot all about it.

Robert All that effort for nothing. Sometimes I feel that there are all these forces acting against me. Like I've got this barrel inside me that gets full of all the bad things that happen. Accidents, injuries, emotional states, Danielle leaving me, cheese. And each of them fills it just that little bit more, until it overflows, and I end up freaking out or scratching all night. It's no good, Nige, I can't go on any more. Did I tell you Danielle left me? It was just a note on a Kit-Kat wrapper, I mean ... ten years.

Nigel Now look, you're making one huge mountain out of your problems. Let's divide them into smaller piles and look at them one by one, set yourself goals you can achieve. How long has it taken you to get this bad?

Robert I don't know, six years, seven years. Since I got into comedy.

Nigel Right, so, how do you expect to get rid of it in one week? It's been going on so long it's become chronic. I'm receiving your pain here, and it feels acute, but actually the problem is chronic.

Robert What the Eddie Izzard are you talking about?

Nigel Well, listen, it's quite simple. There's a

difference between chronic and acute illness. Acute illness comes on very strongly, then either goes away or gets worse. Chronic illness creeps up on you, it can go on over a long period of time and become part of you.

Robert What about ulcers?

Nigel Well, they could be considered chronic in that you have to live with them for years, but then they suddenly burst and you have to go into hospital and then I suppose they're acute. Oh, I don't know! Where's our food?

Robert I had seventeen colds in a row once. But I think that was a way of trying to stop myself pressurising Danielle into having sex all the time.

Nigel Is this Danielle you're talking about Danielle Swinton? The actress?

Robert Yes. She writes now.

Nigel Mmm. And then you went on to play this character that has no penis?

Robert Look, do you have to go on about that one aspect of my character? We tried to make Kryten a fully rounded robot with complex motives and actions.

Nigel Yeah. And no penis.

Robert Oh waaaoooooowwwwww, I'm being hassled maaaan. Oh wow, this is so heaveeeee.

Nigel   Yes, alright. Neil was just an acting job, you know.

Robert. I thought you were doing it live on stage for years before *The Young Ones*.

Nigel   Yes, but that doesn't necessarily mean I based him on myself.

Robert   Doesn't necessarily meant it. But you did, didn't you?

Nigel   Okay, I'll stop going on about the rubber, if you promise not to say heaveeeee again.

Robert   Okay . . . hippy.

Nigel   And don't call me that.

Kelly arrives with two glasses, a large bottle of water and a cappuccino on a tray.

Kelly   Here's your water.

Robert   Thanks, Kelly.

Nigel   Sorry to be a bother, Kelly, but we ordered two teas, I think. Didn't we?

Robert   I wanted a tea, I thought you wanted a coffee.

Kelly   You always have a cappuccino.

Nigel   I know. But today, for some reason, it's tea.

Kelly   It's definitely two teas, then.

Robert Actually, now you mention it, I think tea is going to be altogether too milky for me.

Nigel   You could have it black.

Robert It's too bitter, too clingy to the back of the throat. Orange juice, that's what I really want.

Kelly   So, one tea, one orange juice.

Nigel   Thank you.

Robert Oh God. Kelly, please wait just a moment. I think I'm going to change my mind. No, I seem to be alright.

Kelly. Can I get on with my job, then?

Robert Yes. Sorry, sorry. Sorry.

Kelly walks away.

Robert. I seem to have totally blown it with her.

Nigel   Why, were you looking for a result?

Robert No! No, not really, I mean, she's nice, I find her interesting, sort of weirdly attractive. I can imagine

living in a fishing village with her, I sort of flashed on
being a Tuna fisherman in Sardinia, living in a little house
overlooking the bay, living a simple life, Kelly waiting on
the foreshore with our kids as I came back from the seas,
tanned and muscular, with the catch. Big shiny tuna, tons
of it, slippery in the hold.

Nigel   So you barely noticed her, then.

Robert   Oh God. It's so hopeless. I tried to change
myself for years, you know, tried to stop being a lech. It's
no good. I'm a bloody lech. I just lech after about thirty
percent of all women, all the time. No matter what.

Nigel   That sounds like a very conservative estimate.
What about the other seventy percent?

Robert   I never thought about them, isn't that terrible?
I have to find a way of stopping being like this. So I
thought, I'll go to therapy and find out what's at the root
of it all. And then I think, why bother? Do I really want
to lift the lid on all that? I'm not denying it's a cesspit
down there, I'm not in denial.

Nigel   Not that you'd know if you were.

Robert   Wouldn't I? Oh, shit.

Nigel   Sorry, go on.

Robert   It was like that with Danielle. I couldn't tell
her what my real fantasies were, and gradually more and
more got put under the lid. That's when I start to find

myself behaving in a peculiar way because I'm denying all of the grubby side of me. It happens every time, and then I meet somebody new, and I think it's going to be different and I find myself making the same mistakes, repeating the same patterns with the next person, and the next one.

Nigel   So you became a sort of serial monogamist did you?

Robert   I don't do serial monogamy, I do serial heartbreak. I do serial you-know-you're-going-to-mess-up-big-time-so-why-bother-any-more. I never chat women up any more, I just somehow get involved with women who hate me.

Nigel   I think what's happening in your relationships is that you're focused on narcissistically cathected internal objects.

Robert   Oh, that sounds important. What does it mean?

Nigel   Well, it means that you're falling in love with the image of yourself that you've projected onto someone else.

Robert   All I know is, I'm racing along in a relationship and I'm heading for a big row and I can't seem to see the damn thing coming. I just need some rumble strips.

Nigel   Rumble strips?

Robert   Yeah.

Nigel   Well, you've lost me now.

Robert Rumble strips, the bumpy stripes they put across the road to slow you down before you hit a roundabout. Or in my case go round a roundabout far too fast. I need some of those to help me realise that a row is coming up. I just plough straight into them.

Nigel   No wonder you lost your licence.

Robert I never seem to see them coming, and I know I should slow down a bit, take my foot off the accelerator, not always live my love life with the pedal to the metal.

Nigel   But Robert, on the motorway, do you ever actually reduce speed when it says 'reduce speed now'?

Robert No.

Nigel   I thought not. You don't like to be told, do you? You think it would make you feel like a wimp?

Robert Yeah, I suppose so. I know it's stupid but going to therapy seems like a sign of weakness.

Nigel   Look at Charles and Di. A fascinating case. On that *Panorama* interview she told us how dysfunctional she is, how much help she's sought, how she goes to see 'a gender-related relationship counsellor' or something, and at the time it was all seen as a sign of her strength; in the first place that she goes to a therapist, and secondly that she has the strength of character to tell us about it.

Robert Yes, she was marvellous. I've tried not to have fantasies about her, but I have imagined her with very closely cropped hair.

Nigel And yet, that very same week it was revealed that Prince Charles sees a Jungian analyst and has done for many years, and that was seen as a sign of weakness, or of his being unfit to be king.

Robert So, in the very same week you have exactly the same confession from the Prince and from the Princess of Wales.

Nigel Well, similar, but not the same. There is a big difference between analysis and therapy, you know.

Robert So what's the difference?

Nigel Phew! Big one, Robert. Okay, well, let me see. On the whole, therapy is more goal orientated in that it aims to alleviate symptoms, also it tends to be more short-term with fewer sessions per week. Unlike an analyst, a therapist might try to give you a feeling of being supported, helped or at least empathised with.

Robert But is that going to be enough for my problems? What if I need more than that? What if my problems are more complicated? What if we find that I'm total shit and I need a complete psychic make-over?

Nigel Well, Robert, although most therapists nowadays will use some or other of the basic theories of psychoanalysis, pure psychoanalysis itself is a very different animal. It's not so much concerned with curing individual symptoms and current problems as helping you to undergo a profound change in the structure of your personality. Sessions are five times a week, which is a lot, it can go on for years, and its intention is to make you aware of the unconscious workings of your own mind.

Robert Brainwashing.

Nigel Not at all. It's more autonomous than that.

Robert So it's like washing your own brain.

Nigel I suppose you could almost say that. No, it's more like trimming your own brain, dyeing it a different colour, adding pockets and putting in shoulder-pads or something.

Robert Hmmmm. I should try not to see it in a washing context then.

Nigel Yes. I think that would help. You see, in analysis you wouldn't be so interested in looking at one specific symptom, say, a fear of spiders for instance, you'd concentrate more on trying to understand the underlying anxieties that it might represent.

Robert Yeah, yeah. Spiders. Like your mum's pubic hair.

Nigel If you insist.

Robert Like all sort of hidden and forbidden, like a glimpse at something you're not meant to see, and the fear hits you in the stomach like a lump hammer, and you want to puke and fill your pants at the same time. That's altogether clearer now.

Nigel   But, as I said, there's a grey area in the middle . . .

Robert Oh shit, I knew it.

Nigel   . . . where analytical techniques are used in therapy. This is the big growth industry. Psychoanalytical psychotherapy. It's a bloody mouthful, isn't it? But that's actually what a lot of people are practising these days. There are so many different schools of thought. You've got transactionals, you've got transpersonals, you've got personal-constructs, there's psychosynthesis, there's the person-centreds, there's humanistic therapy and there's existential therapy. Not to mention group work, gestalt and rebirthing. Actually, humanistic is transpersonal, I mustn't confuse you.

Robert God, I'm glad I came to you first. I can see that the world of psychoana-therap-psycho-business, or whatever you called it, is as complicated as one of those computer manuals. You know, where you're better off getting the guy to come around to show you how to switch the damn thing on.

Nigel   Good analogy. I haven't even got a CD player, probably couldn't even open the box it came in. But, Robert, it really isn't that complex. The psychoanalytical psychotherapies are partly like therapy, as in counselling, i.e. being given advice, but also partly like analysis in that they tend to use the theories of the unconscious, i.e. lifting the lid on your inner motives and workings. So you might end up going once or twice a week for a couple of years, or less. Or more, of course.

Robert So, there's a whole range of stuff, and I can choose which one to go to depending on how big a change I want to make to my life or, well, to my being?

Nigel   If only. You see sometimes, therapy patients actually manage to achieve profound changes in the structure of their personality, whereas someone who's been in analysis for eighteen years might not move an inch.

Robert So it's a bit of a wank.

Nigel   I suppose it must depend on the person and the therapist or analyst involved.

Robert Hey, wow. I'm making a connection here. No, wait mate. Charles and Di, analysis and therapy. Don't you think it's possible there's a gender distinction between therapy and analysis? Like analysis is for men, and therapy is more a girls' thing?

Nigel   No.

Robert Fair enough.

Nigel   Actually, that really is rather pathetic Robert.

Robert I know. Go on.

Nigel   So you see, the whole thing is fraught with a fascinating multiplicity of choices.

Robert   It all seems so confusing. Isn't there some kind of British Standard 'kite-mark' kind of thing which they all have to belong to before they can practise?

Nigel   This isn't life insurance you know! It's far too complicated for that. How could you expect all the hundreds of organisations and institutions to recognise each other let alone agree on basic principles and qualifications? I mean how would you like to have your parental introjection fixation treated by a New Age psychic Shaman? Because that's what you're saying!

Robert   Am I? You mean they can all say what they like and offer to treat me even if their therapy isn't the right one for me?

Nigel   Absolutely.

Robert   I see, you mean like try Prozac first . . .?

Nigel   Oh, the easy option. Maybe you should have rung your GP instead of me.

Robert   . . . or alchoholics anonymous? Or alcohol? Or anything?

Nigel   Shall we have a bottle of wine with our meal, or a beer or something?

ROBERT'S DIARY
JUNE 15TH 2.15 am

Clouds part, at last some light. I feel so much clearer about what to do after today's meeting with Nige. We just talked and talked. Well, he talked quite a lot, and I'm always told I tend to dominate a conversation, so it was brilliant to learn about listening. I'm a novice. But then it's right he should dominate because he talks such innate sense. He's so calm, he's so centred that eventually even I calmed down and started to think again. I realise if I allow it to work for me, I have got a bit of a brain up there somewhere. Feels like it's floating above the clouds of my madness. That sounds good, doesn't it? I must tell Nige that one. My intelligence is floating above the clouds of the madness that I live in.

I definitely decided that I think I want to try doing therapy for a bit, as opposed to psychoanalysis. Definitely. I think. But I think I'll wait until Nige and I have met up again.

I forgot to get any money out of the machine before meeting him today so I've promised to take him out for a slap-up lunch at The Ivy, and pay for the lot. I don't care about money any more. There's no point having it if you're too doolally to appreciate it.

NIGEL'S DIARY
JUNE 14TH 9.45 pm

*God, I'm knackered. Robert Llewellyn has worn me
out. Listening to other people's problems for hours can
be really draining, and he really did go on and on. He
may say he wants to sort himself out, but it seems to
me that he doesn't have the stamina or the will-power
to really work things through, to find his anger and sit
with it, walk alongside it hand in hand, relish it. It's a
long journey, and there are no quick, easy answers. Of
all people, I should know for Christ's sake.*

*He said he wants to take me to The Ivy next week.
I love The Ivy, but I'd have to lend him some clothes,
and I'd never get them back. Also, what if Paul Jackson
or Tom Gutteridge are in there and see me with
Robert Llewellyn? I'd never work again. I think I'll wear
the Hugo Boss, that's ambiguous enough. It'd better be
towards the end of the week because for some strange
reason, the diarrhoea has returned. I need more sleep.*

3

A RECIPE FOR SUCCESS

Nigel and Robert are browsing in the fresh produce section of a large upmarket supermarket. Robert rips open the plastic packing on some baby sweet corn, and stuffs one in his mouth.

Nigel   Don't eat that. I'm using it tonight in my Mexican *molé*.

Robert What's *molé*?

Nigel   It's a spicy chilli and chocolate dish I'm cooking for my guests.

Robert Oh God. I'm such a failure. You cook dinner for a whole range of top people, while I get a Chinese take-out on my own.

Nigel   Oh Robert, I call them top people, but it's really just that I hate to mix only with people from our profession. I like to mix with all the professions.

Robert I'd be so out of my depth.

Nigel   I know, but honestly, some people who've had an enormous amount of professional success become more normal than they were before they reached the top. What am I saying? Normal! That's awful, because some people who we might call failures in their careers are much more successful than us in the way they run their actual lives ... What am I saying? That's so pretentious. Could you pass the yoghurt? No, the Greek one. No, the one with acidophilus.

Robert But I'm a failure as a top person, *and* I'm a failure in my actual life.

Nigel   You will keep using the blame frame, won't you? Like, 'Why do I have this problem?' or, 'Why am I such a failure?' Why don't you try asking 'how' questions rather than 'why' questions for a change? Like, 'How can I deal with this?' or 'How can I use my strengths?'

Robert But I can never think that clearly. It all just washes over me and I can't cope.

Nigel   Look Robert, why don't you try and see things more in terms of potential and possibilities rather than stumbling blocks and crises.
An incredibly tall, thin, smiling man in a suit with a name badge on his lapel approaches Nigel and Robert.

Liam Hello gentlemen, Mr Planer, welcome to the store. My name's Liam, and I'm your manager today. Is everything alright for you?

Nigel Very much so. I'm having a problem tracking down the Paraguayan nutmeg, though.

Liam It's in the Special Selection aisle. We're very proud of our increased South American product range now, and particularly with our fair trade policy, which I think our customers demand.

Nigel That's great.

Liam You know Stephen Fry comes here a lot, well . . . before . . . you know. So, if you've got any problems . . .

Liam smiles and walks away purposefully.

Nigel Did you see that? The manager comes over to talk to us. Problem, how do we get rid of him? But the thing is to take that problem and turn it into an opportunity, for instance, as a way of discovering the whereabouts of the Paraguayan nutmeg. Firstly, know what you want, secondly be alert, keep your senses open, thirdly, have the flexibility to keep changing what you do until you get what you want. 'Outcome, acuity, flexibility'.[4]

Robert You sound like you've done EST.

Nigel Erhart Seminar Training? No, actually, what I'm talking about is NLP.

Robert What does that stand for?

Nigel It's an interesting thought that if my middle name was Liam, N.L.P. would be my initials.

Robert What is it really?

Nigel George.

Robert What? No, what is NLP? Nice Little Prick? Huh huh huh.

Nigel Neuro Linguistic Programming. It's the art and science of excellence, derived from studying how top people in different fields obtain their outstanding results. It's the study of what makes the difference between the excellent and the average. It also gives rise to a number of extremely effective techniques for education, counselling, business and therapy.[5]

Robert Have you done it, then?

Nigel No, but I've read a book about it. They do this exercise where they divide a group of people into verbal, visual and physical types, and they give each group different coloured cards. They find that while people with the same colour card can communicate easily with each other, people with different coloured cards, say a blue and a red, find it very difficult.

Robert Hey, I think I've done this, in the eighties.

Nigel Well, the object of the exercise is to maximise

personal potential. To help the client, in effect, to have a multicoloured card. Wait a minute, did you say you've done this?

Robert Yes, I went on this course, sat in front of this bloke in a suit. What did he say? Oh yeah, he told me to identify a situation where I wanted to be more resourceful, so for me it was confidence with women, of course. Then I had to find an occasion in my life when I'd had that extra resource, which was quite difficult for me, obviously, and then identify it with a 'physical anchor'. For instance, pinching my left thumb and finger together. This was my anchor, and then by pinching my thumb and finger together I could 'fire' that anchor and access that state whenever I needed it.

Nigel Ah, yes. You were locating your accessing cues.

Robert Yeah, but I wanted to get better, stop being depressed, learn how to sleep without drugs or drink, hold down something resembling a relationship for more than twenty minutes. All they taught me was how to pyramid sell haircare products in a brand-saturated market. I was successful, yes, in their terms. I made a fortune, I had seven cars, a flat in Docklands, a wide-screen Bang & Olufsen telly. Big deal. So I jacked it all in to go into comedy in '88, sold my Aston Martin DB6 to Chris Barrie, he got me a job on *Red Dwarf*, and here I am. No better off than I was when I started. Worse, I haven't got Danielle now.

Nigel Maybe you just didn't go into it deeply enough, Robert. Because there are other accessing cues, for instance the breathing ones. A person who's thinking in visual images will generally speak more quickly and at a higher pitch than someone who's not. Whereas someone who's thinking in sounds will breathe evenly over the whole chest area.

Robert Wey hey.

Nigel I'm sorry, that 'wey hey' has fallen on barren soil. What have I said that could possibly have illicited a 'wey hey' response?

Robert Chest area.

Nigel I think you must have attended the Carry On School of Neuro Linguistic Programming. Now, where's that damn couscous?

Robert Yeah, just like that bloody autohypnosis.

Nigel You've done autohypnosis as well as NLP?

Robert I think that's what it was.

Nigel Well, did you imagine the blackboard with the number 100 written on it, then you imagined wiping that off and writing 99 and so on, gradually getting more and more relaxed?

Robert Yes, but I had to change that because I kept imagining the chalk was breaking, and there was blood on the blackboard. I was going through a difficult stage, it helped me a bit though. It was nice to know you had that little moment of peace once a day. All to yourself. Like a private little garden.

Nigel Oh yes, autohypnosis is all very well and good if you've got hay fever, asthma, arthritis, stress, a build-up of toxins in your body, or generalised nervous tension. But you have to be careful, Robert, that you aren't just masking your problem, not actually dealing with the underlying cause. Remember, like pain itself, a symptom is a warning sign that there is something wrong underneath, in your case very wrong, Robert, and buried very deep, I suspect.

Robert Oh God, I know you're right. Aren't you buying rather a lot of couscous there, Nigel?

Nigel Oh no, I always cook far too much. One never knows who might turn up!

Robert Don't worry, I'm not coming. I know I'm a social disaster.

Nigel Did you ever consider going to couples therapy with this Danielle? You know, Relate or something?

Robert Oh, that. Yeah, well we did try that. They gave us an appointment, eventually, I mean we had to wait four months for it! Then when it came up I had a gig in Glasgow that night, so we couldn't go. Typical. So we read the book instead, which said we had to stand naked in front of each other, sensually stroking each other with chiffon scarves, without actually having sex. But we weren't having sex at the time anyway, so it all seemed a

bit pointless. In the end, it made me think I'd rather split up with Danielle than go through the embarrassment of doing the rest of the exercises in the book with her.

Nigel   Just because Relate used to be called the Marriage Guidance Council doesn't mean their one aim is to keep couples together at all costs. They might have helped you end the relationship in a better way so that you wouldn't be in such a state now. You know, there is such a thing as a good divorce, and a couples therapist might just have helped you and Danielle sort out which direction you were going in. I know it's unfortunate that you had to wait four months, but their resources are always stretched to the limit. But of course, you had the Glasgow gig. Work is work.

Robert Well, it wasn't a paying gig and I did agree to it after we got the appointment. D'you think that means I was scared of facing up to things?

Nigel   Well, Robert. You could have booked an appointment at a convenient time with any number of relationship or psychosexual counsellors, if you'd been willing to pay a bit more for it, that is.

Robert And that's another thing. Paying for it! If I've got a broken ankle, I don't pay for my doctor, do I? Why can't I get treatment for a broken heart and a rampant libido on the NHS?

Nigel   Well, actually Robert, you can get therapy from the National Health Service, but you have to be very sick to get it, and we haven't yet established that your problem warrants taking valuable public funds away from, for instance, the treatment of a highly disturbed psychotic kleptomaniac arsonist, have we?

Robert So are you telling me I'm just some North London, namby-pamby, self-obsessed, bourgeois bastard who's got the time and money to indulge his petty grievances and then has the audacity to claim that his psychic discoveries have some relevance to the rest of society?

Nigel Yes. And that's not necessarily a bad thing. For instance, the three or four sessions that you and Danielle might have needed to really sort you out would only have cost, say, about a hundred and fifty quid for the lot. You spent that on the train fare to Glasgow.

Robert And some. I bought the entire train a drink, because I was so depressed. But what about me? I mean me, here, now! You know, what if we find I need actual analysis and I have to go five times a week, like for five years, so that's fifty quid a session, two hundred and fifty quid a week, that's thirteen thousand a year, Jesus Christ, that's sixty-five fucking thousand pounds!

Nigel Yes, Robert. Almost as much as you spend on cars. Or what Danielle spent on clothes. Errr . . . I mean one assumes she may have spent that on clothes.

Robert No, you're right mate. Who ever heard of a four-hundred-quid blouse? But then it's all those glossy mags and adverts isn't it, they convince you that you want something you don't really need. Hey, I just thought, therapy's like that, isn't it? Isn't it! It's just a glossy magazine advert to convince you to spend sixty-five thousand quid, really, isn't it!?

Nigel   I can see how it would seem like that, especially since some analysts would interpret what you've just said as a defence against making the necessary realisations about your subconscious, Robert, as a resistance. As you say, not facing up to things, like going to Glasgow instead of Relate.

Robert   Well that's handy, isn't it? 'If you want to stop paying me money, that means you're denying stuff, which proves you need help, which means you need to give me more money.' It's like it's addictive, isn't it?

Nigel   There is that worry. But you're confusing a lot of different things here. We're not all living in villages where we can go and see the elders and sort it all out. It's not a perfect world. You can't throw out the whole of Freud's theory of the unconscious just because some people like you, Robert, have addictive personalities.

Robert   Freud really had it sussed then, didn't he? Squeezing every last Austrian schilling out of his clients while he wrote all these papers and books about them. Making a bloody fortune by trapping them on the couch for years and years.

Nigel   No, he didn't actually. Analysis with Freud would most likely have been quite a short-lived affair. Yes, he used a couch, but he didn't tie patients down on it.

Robert   Ooh err.

Nigel   Sometimes it might even just have been a few short walks together.

Robert You mean there was a definite finish to it?

Nigel   The truth is, it was early days and it wasn't something anyone was entirely sure about. In fact Freud wrote a paper called *Analysis, Terminable or Interminable?*[6] trying to discuss this very issue.

Robert Well, that's not very scientific, is it? He couldn't even make up his own mind about it all. And he called himself a Doctor.

Nigel   Yes, some would say his claims to medical and scientific veracity were overblown, indeed it's interesting that when he won the Nobel prize it was for literature, not science or medicine. He himself said that all of his discoveries could be found in the world of literature.

Robert Oh bully for Freud. Oh wow, Freud did this, Freud did that, just because he won the Nobel prize, we've all got to listen to Freud now, have we? What about me? I've got to know all about Freud's theory of the bloody unconscious just because I scratch all night long, have I?

Nigel   If you want to stop scratching.

Robert As far as I'm concerned he's just another dead white male, a pompous patriarchal old git.

Nigel   Oh don't be so old-fashioned, Robert. The

Freud backlash ended in 1982, I mean, yes, okay, a lot of his ideas were crap. I suppose I could always freeze this fifth chicken if it doesn't get eaten.

Nigel balances the fifth chicken on top of the huge pile in his trolley.

Nigel   It's far too soon after Freud to appreciate the true extent of his influence, but he has changed our whole way of thinking, and brought the idea of the unconscious into common use.

Robert   Yeah, but he was sexist wasn't he? And he had a big white beard, so he could hide behind it and have weird fantasies about all the women he treated.

Nigel   I hope you're going to pay for that can of Special Brew, Robert. Yes, he undoubtedly was sexist, it was a hundred years ago after all. But we don't chuck away the idea of universal peace just because Ghandi may have been horrible to his wife. We don't discard all notions of equality just because Karl Marx had an upper-middle-class upbringing.

Nigel moves the trolley towards the checkout queue.

Robert   Aren't you getting any wine, then?

Nigel   I don't buy wine from here. I get it delivered by a specialist club.

Robert picks up a magazine from the rack and flicks through it sloppily.

Nigel   You think you're being very radical accusing
Freud of being sexist, but as far back as 1929 Karen
Horney, a major voice in psychoanalysis, pointed out that
Freud had a bit of a problem with women. What are you
laughing about, Robert?

Robert   Horny. Huh huh huh.

Nigel   It's Horney with an 'e' actually. Look, okay,
imagine a time before Christmas was invented. People
just sat around the tree and did nothing. And then one
day, your grandma thought of the idea of giving you
a present. It was some boring old handkerchiefs, but
because it was the first time, and you'd never had a
present at Christmas before, you were thrilled. Everyone
else thought it was such a good idea that they all started
giving you presents, bigger and better ones, which
you liked more than the handkerchiefs. Next day your
grandma came up to you all sad and asked, 'Don't you
like my present?' And you said, 'Just because I like the
new ones doesn't mean I didn't like your handkerchiefs,
Grandma, and anyway, it was your idea to give presents
in the first place.'[7] So in a sense, your grandma invented
Christmas. Now, Freud's like the grandmother of therapy.

Robert   Yeah, but handkerchiefs are still crap presents.

Robert drops one magazine back in the rack and picks up
Family Circle *magazine.*

Nigel   Don't look in that magazine, Robert.

Robert It's alright, I'm not messing them up, I'll put it back before we go through the checkout.

Nigel No, just don't look in it.

Robert Arrghhh! It's you! Yuk, in a cardigan! What are you advertising? Free-standing barbecue units? Disgusting! And what about the trousers!

Nigel They made me wear those slacks.

Robert Slacks? What the hell are slacks?

Nigel Look, for goodness sake Robert, it's just an advert. We all have to do them. Anyway, it's for an SEF for Allied Dundee.

Robert What's an SEF? Slacks Everyone Fears?

Nigel A Semi Ethical Fund. There's a green clause in it about only selling arms to stable democracies, that sort of thing.

Robert Investments, financial products, that's even worse! And slacks! I DO NOT KNOW THIS MAN. HE WEARS SLACKS FOR MONEY. LOOK!

Robert waves the magazine at bemused shoppers. Nigel snatches it out of his hand, ripping it slightly.

Nigel Robert, will you just shut up. Now I'll have to buy the bloody thing. Look, that advert actually gave me enough money to put on that play last year at the Queen's Head.

Robert I personally think *Wild Swans* would have been better left as a book.

Nigel Yes, well so did most of the critics, but that's beside the point. Anyway Robert, it was you who was complaining about having to pay for therapy. But if you had medical insurance, it's companies like Allied Dundee who would pay for your treatment. Or, they should do.

Robert What, you mean they'd pay sixty-five thousand quid for me to talk to some bloke in a room?

Nigel Or woman. Well, obviously no, but many health insurance policies cover a year or so of therapy, although they are trying to back out of it these days, which is stupid when you think they will happily pay for a week in a special unit with drug treatments ...

Checkout operative (girl) Is this empty can of Special Brew yours, sir?

Nigel ... which would cost far more and wouldn't necessarily be more effective. What? Robert?

Nigel looks around and Robert is nowhere to be seen. Nigel looks down at the revolving product belt as a half-crumpled can of Special Brew slowly turns and spills the remains of its contents onto the checkout till.

Nigel Yes, yes, yes. I'll pay for that.

NIGEL'S DIARY
JUNE 17TH 11.15 am

Rather a lot of molé and couscous left over. Must consider getting a larger freezer. One always expects one guest to cancel, or maybe even two. Still, it was a fun evening. Luckily I managed to stash the trestle table out on the fire escape in time. What a revelation old Mrs Tonkins was, who ever would have guessed she once cleaned for the Jaggers?

Robert is beginning to irritate me, but I know that's just my projective identification. I think he is in quite a bad way and it would be churlish of me not to help, even though he does have some pretty lager-loutish attitudes. In a quiet moment during the evening I almost thought I should ring him, but on the other hand I don't want to frighten him off, because actually I do think I've got something to offer him.

Rather nice to be recognised by that supermarket manager.

ROBERT'S DIARY
JUNE 16TH 11.45 pm

*Just thinking about Nigel is making me depressed.
As I write this, there he is, surrounded by his erudite
friends, having a fabulous dinner party. He's probably
laughing about me, telling all those overdressed men
and women what a tragic case I am. And I bet the
women are just laughing about me, and one of them,
with a long neck with her hair all tied up loose, is
probably running her slender fingers up the thigh of
the man next to her. I bet she gives him fingertip relief
under the table. She probably gives each man relief,
one by one, as she pretends to drop her fork under
the table. Oh Christ, Nigel's right, I really do need help.
What's happening to me? Is this madness? I wonder
if he's gone to bed, could I ring him now? He might
be able to talk me down. Naahh. He wouldn't speak
to me anyway, I've really blown it with him. The way
I behaved in the supermarket today was so stupid.
I would have done that ad if they'd offered it to me.
Mind you, I'd have insisted on a 'no slacks' clause in
the contract. And what's Semi Ethical for fuck's sake?*

THE LIFT

Nigel enters the famous BBC rehearsal rooms in North Acton. This popular building is seven storeys high, on each floor are three large open-plan rehearsal rooms and a string of production offices. On the seventh floor is the BBC's finest subsidised canteen with a rooftop outdoor eating area giving views over twenty miles of West London. In the entrance foyer, Robert is sitting next to the soft drinks dispensing machine looking furtively at Mandy, a uniformed security operative on duty behind the counter.

Mandy   Morning, Mr Planer.

Nigel   Morning, Mandy. Has he been giving you a hard time?

Mandy Who?

Robert Hi, Nige. Thanks for this, I really, you know . . .

Nigel Yeah, yeah, yeah. It's okay. Right, my rehearsals start at two thirty. Let's eat.

Nigel presses the lift button.

Robert Erm, can we take the stairs?

Nigel It's seven floors up!

Robert Yeah, I just had this crazy idea it would be good to go up the stairs today. Huh, stupid really.

Nigel Now look, Robert, breathe deeply. Having trouble with lifts is not something you need to feel bad about. It's curable, we can handle this, and luckily these days it's something I do happen to know something about.

Robert No, no, it's not that I'm agoraphobic or anything.

Nigel You mean claustrophobic, Robert. If you were agoraphobic, you wouldn't have been able to get out of your front door. Don't worry, I know a good way of dealing with this problem.

The lift doors open, they step inside.

Nigel In fact there would be several ways of dealing

with this problem, depending on whether you went for a behaviourist approach or a psychoanalytical approach to therapy. Will you look at me while I'm talking to you?

Robert Sorry.

Nigel The behaviourists wouldn't be interested at all in what's going on inside you, they say that the symptom is the illness. Whereas an analyst, or a psychoanalytical psychotherapist, would say that there is an underlying illness, or disturbance, of which the symptom is an outward manifestation. Behaviourists have a lot of success with monosymptomatic cases like yours, people with phobias or a tangible single problem, because they believe symptoms are not the result of some inner conflict which needs uncovering, but the result of your conditioning. So what they try to do is recondition you, sort of give you a retread. So you see, a behaviourist would say, 'You have an anxiety going into a lift. Fine, mate, let's work on that.' First, by imagining it, maybe drawing a picture of it, doing relaxing breathing exercises all the time. And then, over a number of sessions, you'd gradually work up to going near a lift, still staying calm. Then, maybe go and stand in one and get straight out again, then try going up just one floor, and build it up slowly so that you're no longer scared of going in lifts. End of problem . . .

Robert Yeah, but Nige, that's not quite what I meant.

Nigel . . . whereas an analyst, as opposed to a behaviourist, would encourage you to see your symptom as an indicator. To use the symptom to uncover your own inner workings. For instance, you would look at your lift phobia, or your dreams or your other fears over a long period of time to enable you to a reach a deeper understanding of yourself, to help make deep changes to the way your personality functions.

The lift doors open.

Robert Thanks Nige, but I don't have a lift phobia.

Nigel It's nothing to be ashamed of.

Robert No really, I just wanted to go up the stairs because there's this woman working on the fifth floor called Rebecca who's a stage manager. I don't know her but I've had a lot of fantasies about her, sort of revolutionary-guerilla-fighter-in-the-El-Salvadorian-jungle ones. You know, with her with one of those fatigue vests on, a bit sweaty, quite tight, carrying a Kalashnikov rifle with a handwoven shoulder strap, and you look at her hands and you know she's holding a grenade, and you think that if only you could help her cause, she could cradle a baby's bottom with those lovely hands . . . my baby.

Nigel Now that *is* something to be ashamed of.

They pick up two trays and join the queue in the canteen.

Nigel Well, Robert, if you haven't got an inner conflict, you bloody well should have.

Robert You're right, I'm so libidinous, all I think about is women, I force them into fantasy situations which have nothing to do with their real lives. All I want to do is chaste around after women.

Nigel   I can read you like a cheap paperback. Did you hear yourself just then? You said 'chaste' when I think you meant 'chase'. That's a classic example of a Freudian slip.

Robert   Freudian slit more like. Huh huh huh.

Nigel   Are you having asparagus spears with your pitta bread? No? Listen Robert, if I was a Freudian, we could take your little slip of the tongue just then and use it to throw possible light on what's really going on inside you, and find out why you are such a deeply conflicted and raddled individual. For instance, you claim that being too randy is your problem and this seems to make you feel guilty and shitty about yourself. As if you were some ball of pure testosterone which ought to be chained down, and yet you have never assaulted or raped anyone, you've only ever had one girlfriend and you play a character with no penis. You're actually quite a nice guy. You were faithful and loyal to Danielle, weren't you?

Robert   Physically, yes, but emotionally I was a complete bastard.

Nigel   So when you said 'chaste' just now, it could have been a pointer to your inside need for security and monogamous stability, which you are denying because you are afraid of not appearing masculine enough. You think your problem is that you're too much of a Don Juan, but really you're a Leporello who thinks he ought to be a Don Juan.

Robert Who's Leporello?

Nigel Don Juan's sidekick. The earthy figure who embodies the eternal envy of the slave for his master. You know, Sancho Panza? Fry and Laurie? Abbot and Costello?

Robert Wow, so I've got a Leporello complex. Brilliant!

Nigel There's no such thing, I was just trying to offer one interpretation.

They reach the till. Robert pushes his overloaded tray next to Nigel's salad and mineral water.

Till operative Are these together?

Robert Yes. Sorry Nige, you know, the cash machine, um, there was a queue, and, um, I forgot my card.

Nigel pays for lunch. They sit down at a table near Sting.

Nigel Hi, Gordon.

Sting Hi Nigel, how's it going?

Nigel Very well, thanks. D'you know Robert?

Sting No.

Robert and Nigel turn to face each other and start to eat.

Robert Oh God, how come you know him? What's he doing here?

Nigel He's playing King Lear for BBC Two.

Robert I've never liked him. I can't see it. Danielle used to cream her knickers over him. You know what they say about him, he has three trucks on tour, one for the band, one for the lights, one for his ego.

Nigel Yes, I've heard that one.

Robert Oh, come on, Nige. They're all like that, rock stars, ego ego ego. Don't you think, Nige? Really. I mean, what's it all about?

Nigel Well, clearly the ego has something to do with it.

Robert Oh, come on! Look at the way they present themselves, they really believe the world revolves around them. He's just a balding ex-teacher with a massive ego . . . or am I using the term wrongly? Nige . . .?

Nigel Technically speaking, you are using it wrongly. But it doesn't matter, Robert. Look, we didn't come here to talk about Gordon's ego. You rang me.

Robert Actually, I rang you because my life is virtually dangling from the merest thread and I feel like I won't be able to get through another day. I thought, since you're my friend now, you might be able to help me, but never mind. I'll be okay. I'll just carry on using all the wrong terms and people like Sting will just laugh at me. I bet he knows what ego really means.

Nigel   Robert, you strike me as someone full of dark imaginings and chaotic longings who has a cauldron full of seething desires and deep instinctual urges bubbling away just beneath the surface.

Robert You know I have.

Nigel   But, have you ever actually woken up with blood on your hands? I mean, how many of these grubby fantasies have you actually acted on?

Robert That's the whole problem. I can control myself, just, but it's so exhausting.

Nigel   Well, there you are then. That's your ego.

Robert What, the steaming sexy cauldron of molten spunk fire?

Nigel wipes some of Robert's taramasalata from his chin.

Nigel   No. That's your id. Think of it like a man on horseback who has to hold in check the superior strength of the horse.[8] Your id is the horse, your ego is the rider. The ego is the conscious organisational part of your personality. It's what you mean when you say the word 'I'. But there's so much more to you than that, isn't there? Where does 'I' go when you're asleep, when you dream, when you think about Rebecca the stage manager?

Sting stands up and passes their table. He leans across Nigel and puts his hand on Robert's shoulder.

Sting   I've just realised who you are. You're that bloke in the mask, Kryten. From *Red Dwarf*, isn't it? You're brilliant, I love your stuff. So funny. Brilliant. Keep on doing it.

Robert   Oh, right. Um, thanks . . . er . . . Gordon. No, really.

Sting walks away studying a heavy script.

Robert   God, amazing, did you see that Nigel? Actually I always liked 'Message in a Bottle'.

Nigel   Sure. So, that's the id and the ego. There's another part of the mind which is called the super ego which is sort of like your conscience. It's the bit of you that can look at yourself and be critical. If you like, you could say it's your internalised parental figure, or what you imagined authority meant when you were a little kid.

Robert   God, does that mean Sting's got a super ego?

Nigel   Boy, has he got one! His saved the rain forest.

Robert   Actually, I quite like that album he did, '*The Dream of The Green Turtles*'.

Nigel   They were blue, but never mind. Listen Robert, I haven't finished, the whole point is that the ego is constantly having to negotiate between the totally different natures of the id and the super ego. The id is wild and passionate, and the super ego is cool and controlling, so your poor ego is caught in the middle trying to keep them both happy, whilst at the same time trying to help you cope with real life outside. You said it was exhausting, well, you're right. It's the skill with which your ego manages this task which decides how disturbed you are.

Robert So I've got a crap ego, is that what you're saying?

Nigel Well, yes. You asked me to help. Look, your dark and passionate id was jealous of Sting and wanted to kill him. Your super ego made you sit down and eat your lunch instead, because killing him would be uncool, and your ego compromised by making you slither and crawl up to him just now when he acknowledged your existence.

Robert So how disturbed am I?

Nigel Look, the thing analysis and therapy have in common, if they're working, is that you can find a safe place where revealing the grubbier side of you is not going to have any consequences outside that room.

Robert I've always wanted to be honest about my grubby side, almost as a political act. I refuse to be a repressed Victorian English male. I've shouted at people at parties, 'I've done so and so!' and their noses turn up because they really want to talk about house prices.

Nigel   Keep your voice down.

Robert Sorry.

Nigel   Just shouting your conscious fantasies at innocent people is not what I meant. It's what's underneath that needs to be revealed. For instance, your slip of the tongue just now, your 'chaste women' might be used as a window by an analyst to shed light on what's going on in your unconscious. Or to make your ego aware of what's really going on in your id.

Robert Surely being with my mates is safe enough? I feel safe with you, Nige, you're my mate now. Can't I just talk to you?

Nigel   Well, the only problem with a friend is that they may have problems of their own, or ulterior motives in listening to you. They may have a set of religious or political beliefs which force them to advise you in a certain way, or they may just fancy you, or your partner. Whoever they are, there will be some kind of agenda.

Robert Did you ever meet Danielle?

Nigel   Once. How do you know you can trust your friends? How do you know you can trust yourself? In fact, in every encounter you make in your life, in every conversation, you will be having some kind of effect on the other person, and they, however understanding they may seem, will have some kind of influence over you.

Robert What year were you at the Sheffield Crucible?

Nigel   1987. Well, the idea in a psychoanalytical situation is that, for once, the buck stops. For the first time in your life you are going to talk to someone who does not have their own personal axe to grind, someone who will not project their own personal shit back onto you.

Robert Oh. I don't think she was there in '87.

Nigel   You can project all your crappiest thoughts, all those sneaky ways you manage to blame the world, or your parents, for your own shortcomings, and the analyst or therapist will just sit there saying uninflected things like, 'And how does this make you feel?'

Robert Do they really say that!

Nigel   They're not passing judgement, not really doing anything. It's like shouting at a brick wall, until gradually you run out of steam, and find yourself confronting yourself for the first time. Like a mirror in which it takes three years to recognise yourself. That's the idea anyway.

Robert So you think I'm the sort of person who needs the absolute full-on, five-times-a-week, intensive Freudian analysis. I mean, the vindaloo, not the chicken korma.

Nigel   Not necessarily. Look, if this bit of old lettuce is behaviourism, and this apple crumble and custard over here is Freudian analysis, then all of these cold chips in between represent the wide range of possible other avenues to explore. This salt cellar is psychoanalytical psychotherapy, which uses analytical theory in a more relaxed therapeutic setting. And this fork down this end is a gestalt fork, which might get involved in more trauma confrontation and group work.

Robert What's this bit of sweet corn next to the crumble?

Nigel That's Kleinian corn and it's very cross. Kleinian analysts are into envy, gratitude, and infantile rage against the mother's breast.

Robert Where am I, then?

Nigel Well, bearing in mind everything you've told me so far, you're this ashtray.

Robert So where should I put it, next to the lettuce or the salt cellar?

Nigel I can't possibly say. It has to be *your* choice, I'm just laying out your options in as clear and graphic a way as possible.

Robert I'm just looking at a load of bits of food on the table, I've forgotten which is which.

A woman runs up to their table with a clipboard.

Woman Hello, Mr Planer. We need you now, if that's okay.

Nigel Goodness, is it two thirty already? Good Lord, it's quarter to three!

Woman We're in 503.

The woman runs away. Nigel stands up.

Nigel What's the matter, Robert?

Robert Omigodomigodomigod! It's her! It's Rebecca, it's Rebecca Dulcinea Del Taboso.

Nigel Oh, that's your Rebecca. Nice girl, but nothing to write home about. Look, you've had a lot to think about today. Put it all out of your mind, take a walk, have a bath, watch some telly, eat a curry. Whatever it is you do. I have to go. So sorry. I hope what I've said has been of some help, and listen, call me any time, middle of the night, I mean it.

Nigel grasps Robert's elbow in comradely fashion.

Robert You couldn't lend us a couple of quid could you, just for the tube and a can of Special Brew?

NIGEL'S DIARY
JUNE 27TH 11.03 pm

Rehearsals finished early, for some reason they like what I'm doing! New director not quite on top of it. Had lunch with Robert, who insisted on turning up at North Acton of all places, but for some strange reason I didn't mind. I think for the first time I'm actually helping someone, which feels really good. It's so incredible that something as simple as actually being needed by someone can have such a beneficial effect on me.

I think Robert had some genuine insights into his personality today. Maybe as a second career I should think of being a therapist myself. Actor, writer, painter, psychoanalyst. Mmmm.

Don't think he suspects about me and Danielle. Still, it was a long time ago.

ROBERT'S DIARY
JUNE 27TH 8.45 pm

When I was talking to Sting today, he really made things clear for me. To use your super ego to save the world's rain forest, now there's a potent argument in favour of Jungian psychoanalysis. But I think it's my id that's the problem, that's the out-of-control bit. Suddenly needed to write it all down. Got out the old computer, and the screen came on and there it was! It's DOS, isn't it? Therapy would be like calling up my id so I can see it. Like getting DOS on the screen so you can rewrite your program a bit. Spent seventeen hours typing in anything I could think of about my past, like a sort of free-floating association. Just loads and loads of stuff about being a kid, and Mum and Dad, and when Spot died. I wonder if it would be possible to write a piece of software that people could use to psychoanalyse themselves?

That's just typical of me, though, my mechanistic way of looking at feelings and human relationships. Danielle was right, I'm just like a robot, that's why I got the job on **Red Dwarf.**

Nigel has been okay, but he totally lost me when he put those chips all over the table, I really wanted to eat them but I was too embarrassed.

NIGEL'S DIARY
JULY 18TH 2.30 am

Robert didn't show today, I hope he's okay. Bit pissed off waiting for an hour and a half in the Kentucky Pancake. Feel a bit like Frankenstein's monster, every time I come out of my shell, or make a move towards someone, they run away.

Got soaked in the rain waiting for a cab.
Florence not talking, what's new?
Diarrhoea back.
Why is it always me?

ROBERT'S DIARY
JULY 19TH 10 am

Sitting in Wales in the rain, working out how I got to this point in my life. Brought my laptop with me and stayed in the B & B all night, working out a formula for my childhood.

It's this. RL^^56CL>\ \{2+Spot)–//–>.

It's that clear.

5

BOUNDARIES

Nigel is lying prone on a high bed in a small room. The walls are decorated with two complex diagrams of the human body with lines drawn along them, Chinese writing abounds.

Nigel is undergoing acupuncture at a Camden Town clinic. He has needles inserted all over his body, including one in his tongue and another in his penis. He is feeling exposed but relaxed. The acupuncturist exits the room quietly. Nigel tries to feel the energy being released through his body. Suddenly the door bangs open and Robert enters.

Robert Nige, I've just had this amazing revelation! Listen, it's all to do with the way my mum and dad ignored me on my third birthday. I had to tell you as you hadn't rung for two days.

Nigel   Wrobburd. Whad are you thoing in my threatmenth wroomth?

Robert   I can't remember for certain that they ignored me, but if they did, and it would be the sort of thing they'd do, then the trauma of that would have created a displacement in my id, wouldn't it? Which my super ego would have converted onto women. I just had to tell you, I almost feel like you are my mum and dad now. So I have to tell you because you listen, they never listened, but you listen. I felt so good, I was going to join a gym to get fit again, sweat it out, but then I thought I needed to tell you first.

Nigel   Wrobburd. Thith ith a bith of an impothithioth you thnow.

Robert   Blimey, you've got a pin in your tongue! Can I use your towel, my hair got really wet as I walked here from the tube. Anyway, I just couldn't wait to tell you about it. I was up all last night working it out. Did you know you've got a needle in your willy too? I've never seen that before, what did the acupuncturist say that was for? Kinky.

Nigel   I thinth we ougth to taw abow boundrieth Wrobburd.

Robert   I'm sorry, I can't quite make out what you're saying.

Nigel pulls out the tongue needle causing considerable

discomfort. He sits on the edge of the treatment bed and breathes deeply.

Nigel   Robert. Let's talk about boundaries.

Robert   D'you think I need boundaries, then? Is that what I need?

Nigel   And some! Let's just go back a few steps. How did you know I was here?

Robert   Well, I rang you at home, you weren't there. I rang your agent's office, they said you might be with your aunt, I rang her, she hasn't seen you since last Christmas and said could you ring, but she told me to ring this woman called Florence, so I rang Florence, she said she thought you still came here every now and then to try and cure your diarrhoea, so I rang them here and they wouldn't tell me anything, so I knew you were here. I didn't know you got diarrhoea.

Nigel   Yes, it's something I try and keep to myself.

Robert   The trouble is, what if I decide to go and see someone and it turns out to be a woman, and she's a silver-haired woman in a white coat? Do they wear white coats? I'd be done for if she walked in wearing a white coat with short cropped grey hair and her delicate hands were fondling my file. And I . . .

Nigel   I think maybe for you, Robert, a male practitioner might be the order of the day.

Robert Yes, you're right. This is why I need to talk to you. But what if revealing all my grubby side to a man makes me long for him in some sort of twisted, older-brother, arm-around-the-shoulder, soft-cuddle-up-against-a-hard-chest thing?

Nigel Well, it's interesting you should say that, Robert, because of course if you were in classical analysis that kind of longing would be something that you might well experience, and it wouldn't be such a bad thing, provided it were not reciprocated. And that's because over a period of time in analysis something called transference usually develops, and it's a useful tool.

Robert Wey hey.

Nigel What have I said now? Transference? Analysis? Oh, tool. Very funny. D'you want me to explain this or not? Okay, for instance, just now, you said I was like your mum and dad, didn't you? Well, that's a sort of transference, it happens all the time. We all do it, we endow other people, particularly close friends or lovers, with significance that has more to do with our own feelings about how we were treated in the past. Well, the idea is that if you were in analysis you'd do this transference onto the analyst as much as you liked, but he wouldn't do it back to you.

Robert Or she.

Nigel Maybe you're right, maybe it would be good for you to see a woman, Robert. In terms of transference she might sort you out once and for all. You could have all the cropped-grey-hair, sicko-chauvinist, white-coat, file-fondling fantasies you wanted.

Robert Could I?

Nigel If it made you happy, Robert. Because they would bounce right off her and come back and smack you in the face.

Robert That doesn't sound very nice.

Nigel They're not interested in being nice, or in reassuring you, or giving you advice, all they're interested in doing is helping you to become aware of what's going on in your unconscious mind. You say whatever comes into your head, they listen and interpret it. That's it. It's very formal, they would try to remain very detached. You'd lie on a couch and you wouldn't even see the analyst, he or she would be sitting behind you. The only time you'd have physical contact would be when you'd shake hands the first time you meet.

Robert Oh, yeah, I see. But if I was an analyst and, say, one of my patients was a very attractive young girl in one of those slightly clingy summer dresses whose problem was inappropriate flirtation with older men, I mean, I couldn't stay detached. Could you?

Nigel Well, you're right, counter-transference can be a problem.

Robert It all sounds really kind of cold and horrible and clinical.

Nigel It was you who said you wanted the full-on, five-days-a-week, classical Freudian number! There's hundreds of other types of therapy available in which the therapist will empathise with your plight, give you support through the process and maybe, Robert, even be nice to you.

Nigel gets up and reaches for a silk dressing-gown.

Robert Are there?

Nigel This is what I tried to explain to you last time! You don't listen to anything I say, do you? Yeeaaaawwwwww!

Robert Nige, I meant to say, remember you've still got that pin in your willy.

Nigel I kneeeaaaaooooooww!!!! So, look. It's fairly obvious, isn't it, that you're not going to flourish in such a rigid setting. We may have to accept that you need a therapist who's warmer and gentler and can see the world from your point of view. Someone who could reassure you and help you believe in your own self-worth.

Robert Are you winding me up? I could go and see my mum for that, and get my laundry done.

Nigel Well, no. Actually, I'm serious. There's a different school of thought that doesn't go along with the whole theory of the unconscious and transference. It's called the humanistic approach, or the human potential movement. They believe in creating a facilitating climate where genuineness, acceptance and empathy are all present. They believe that at the very bottom of every person, in the very darkest corner of their soul, is the word 'positive.'

Robert Oh, yuk! Tell me, would the densest conglomeration of these people, by any chance, be found in an area roughly defined within a boundary slightly east of Hawaii, slightly south of Alaska, north of the Mexican Baja peninsula and just a little west of the Rockies?

Nigel   You mean California? Absolutely right.

Robert Oh, stroke my crystals, man.

Nigel   Person-centred therapy, started by Carl Rogers at the Esalen Institute in California is probably the only major voice in the broad church of psychotherapy, apart from behaviourists, which didn't originate in Europe. Actually he started out as a Christian Evangelist in the YMCA. Look, Robert, you're having a problem at the moment making up your mind about what therapy to choose, aren't you? Why can't you just do what feels right for you? I'll tell you why you can't, because you don't believe that you're essentially trustworthy in yourself, do you? Now, a Rogerian would help you with that, because they believe that when an activity 'feels' as though it is valuable or worth doing, it *is* worth doing.[9] A Rogerian would have an 'unconditional positive regard' for you.

Robert I don't want to do any growth-workshop, role-playing, bellowing-'who, who, who'-and-hyperventilating-in-an-orange-shirt stuff. I did all that in the seventies. In the darkest recesses of my soul it doesn't say 'positive', it says 'blue vein shuffle'.

Nigel Oh Robert, a typically hysterical reaction. That's gestalt you're talking about. If you're going to slag off people's life work, at least get the right ones. Fritz and Laura Perls conceived the idea of gestalt through group weekends which were confrontative and anti-intellectual. They devised many of the exercises which are now so often used in all sorts of therapies. Such as, talking to chairs in a role-playing dramatisation of your early life, beating pillows as a re-creation of inner conflicts, and jumping up and down screaming your mother's name repeatedly. And you pooh-pooh them because, yes, okay, they probably did wear rope sandals. But you're seeing rope sandals outside the context of the cultural mélange from which they burst. And what the hell does 'blue vein shuffle' mean? . . . Oh God, Robert. Typical.

A woman in a white coat enters with a box of steaming needles. Robert curls into himself like a hedgehog.

Anna Oh, hello? This is a private treatment room, you know.

Nigel No, it's okay, Anna. I know him. Sort of.

Anna I think you should lie back down, Mr Planer. And what's happened to the needle in your tongue?

Robert holds it up.

Robert   It's over here. D'you want me to bung it back in?

Anna   No, it's alright. I was coming in to remove it anyway.

Robert   So, having these pins in, does it work? Does it stop you shitting yourself?

Anna   Well, acupuncture only works on about fifty percent of people, but when it does work, the results can be staggering. And we're not quite sure yet about Mr Planer's response, are we?

Robert   How many sessions have you had, Nige?

Nigel   Seventeen.

Robert   Right, but it's a load of old bollocks really, isn't it? All that stuff about energy paths through your body which get blocked. I can't see them or feel them. What about kaolin and morphine? Or a cork?

Nigel   Okay. Try and imagine these energy paths, or meridians, more as a map of how the human body interacts with itself. To actually try and see them would be as stupid as standing on the equator looking for a line in the sand.

Anna   That's very good, that really is a clear description, Mr Planer. Could I use that in my book?

Nigel Oh, well . . . I'm sure that would be okay, really. Yes, of course.

Anna That little fellow needs a tweak, and I'll leave you here for another ten minutes.

Nigel Oooww! Yes, that's fine.

She goes. Nigel lies back languorously.

Nigel Marvellous. Yes, you see, Robert, acupuncture is based on one of the most ancient systems of medicine in the world, you shouldn't knock it. The idea of the meridians and pressure points is generally accepted in Western medicine at last, as well as being used in thousands of different types of treatment. John Prescott is reputed to have his own private foot reflexologist for God's sake. Massage to specific points on the soles of the feet is known to be beneficial to the various organs and parts of the body to which they are joined via the meridians, which you so casually dismissed just now.

Robert I know! Why did I do that? I said acupuncture was a load of bollocks. I said 'shit yourself', in front of her. I soiled the sanctuary of her practice room. She hates me.

Nigel And shiatsu, that's another one. It's a holistic massage technique based on the acupressure system. You know, Robert, maybe I've been wrong about you all along. I assumed in my rigid and logical way that what you wanted was what you said you wanted, a talking therapy. I shouldn't have listened to you, I should have obeyed my instincts. Looking back, I knew all along. I had this feeling when you first rang that all you needed was something to relax you and calm you down. I mean, look at you, a woman comes into the room and you're a mass of physical twitches and knots. Have you thought about the Alexander technique, or aromatherapy?

Robert God, you're right, I *am* twisted up. D'you think she noticed?

Nigel Why don't you stop worrying about what she does or doesn't think and do some work on yourself? You know, the more I think about it, you might really benefit from something like Alexander, for instance. It might help you to change the bad habit that you've got into of letting your emotional state affect the way you use your body, and the way you use your body affect your emotional state. It'd be very rejuvenating, and it's something you learn to do for yourself.

Robert Isn't aromatherapy the one where you lie naked in a darkened room and a woman rubs oils all over you?

Nigel That's very sexist, Robert. We're not talking about massage parlours here although, saying that, the one time I tried aromatherapy it did have the effect of relaxing me into a state of mild tumescence, which soon passed of course, as I experienced the soothing effect of the essential oils.

Robert So it's better than having a pin in it, then.

Nigel Oh dear, I can see you're going to have to be

forced into relaxing. You're going to need something really heavy. Rolfing it is, then.

Robert What's that one?

Nigel This is the one that will floor even you. As they would say in Afro-Caribbean circles, you will be 'mash up bad'. You see, the idea is that your muscles are resting in a sort of sheath which joins them to the ligament. If you imagine that sheath like a bit of cling film around some steak, over the years as you become tense in certain areas, and your posture deteriorates, the sheath buckles up. You know, the way cling film does, and sticks to itself? Rolfing is a deep tissue massage which aims to smooth out that puckered sheath and restore balance and alignment to your perversely twisted form, Robert. It can be very painful, they use elbows and knuckles to get right down in between the muscle and the bone and it usually takes about ten sessions. I've been rolfed.

Robert You mean a big Afro-Caribbean pummels your sheaths for an hour?

Nigel Trust you to get completely the wrong end of a non-existent stick. I was just trying to show you the possible choices if you decided to go down a psychophysical route. A more hands-on way of dealing with your problems.

Robert No, but I'm there, Nige. I'm on the couch, I'm being physically healed, I'm working on my mind–body interface, I'm serious about it, but what happened to all that 'transference' thing you were talking about? I liked that bit.

Nigel   No, that's the talking therapies, Robert! You're muddling two completely different approaches here. Obviously transference only works if the analyst makes him- or herself into a blank screen onto which you could project all your early experiences. Clearly, that's not going to happen with someone who's invaded your personal body space so much as to actually put their hands on you. It's a different kind of boundary.

Robert   Ah, that's it. Brilliant, Nige! I get it. On the one hand, there's all the Freudian don't-touch-don't-look-just-transfer business, and on the other side is the oil-up, tickle, rub and mash school of thought.

Nigel   Well, yes . . .

Anna enters.

Anna   Right, you're done, Mr Planer.

She starts removing needles.

Nigel   But this is where it gets really interesting, Robert. Because there is, or rather was, a whole other branch of psychotherapy which basically went along with most of Freud's ideas, but ditched the transference concept, thereby allowing them to become involved in a physical way with their patients. A lot of what they did has since been discredited. In fact Wilhelm Reich, the founder of the movement and an early disciple of Freud's was finally and fatally persecuted by the US government. Ow!

Anna Sorry, Mr Planer. You can get dressed now, and would your friend like a cup of tea?

Robert No, thanks. I'm perfectly lubricated.

Anna Okay.

She goes. Nigel gets dressed.

Robert Damn! Why did I say that? I always blow it, lubricated! I've never said lubricated in my life! She was only offering me tea, she wasn't trying to push me into sex. I was projecting onto her and transferring all my fears into a tea-rejection situation. God, poor woman. Why do I have to be so nervous and scared that the only way I can deal with it is to imagine that she hated me?

Nigel Could you pass my coat? Thank you. You see, the thing about Wilhelm Reich's ideas is that some of them have been embraced by all those other types of therapies we've talked about today, even though at the time he was rejected by just about everybody: the psychoanalysts for being too political, the communists for being too pyschological, the Nazis for being a menace to fascism, and the Americans for making a box out of tin, in which he claimed to be able to harness the energy of the human orgasm to turn on a light bulb! It's generally now accepted that he was probably several sandwiches and a pickled cucumber short of a full lunch-box. But basically, the idea came from Reich that a therapist could press, prod and knead blocked muscles and emotions as a way to achieving psychological health.

Robert Well, that doesn't sound too mad. Maybe he was just ahead of his time.

They leave the acupuncture treatment room.

Nigel   I'm sure he was, but it's a trifle hard to take someone seriously who based his massage technique on the phylogenetic premise that we are all descended from earthworms.[10] So, he would open up blockages from the forehead down through the eyes, throat, shoulders, stomach and perineum to the genitals, which he considered central to his work. You see, he believed that neurosis is caused exclusively by the inhibition of sexual discharge, and that the only way to total health is through complete orgasm. And to save you the trouble, Robert, wey hey! How much do I owe you, Anna?

Anna   You're paid up to date, Mr Planer.

Nigel   Twenty years ago, for instance, Anna here might have been running any number of weekend workshops using some kind of Reichian sexual biofunctional technique. So one could say that Reich helped to open the door for these more holistic approaches to healing.

Anna   Actually, Mr Planer, twenty years ago I was six, and I do have a degree in physiology from Cambridge.

Robert It was nice to meet you, Anna. I'm sorry I barged in earlier on, sort of stepped over your boundaries. See you again, maybe.

Anna   I'm here Thursdays and Saturdays. 'Bye.

NIGEL'S DIARY
JULY 20TH 2 am

I was really disappointed with Robert today. He doesn't turn up when I'm expecting him, then suddenly shows up in the privacy of my treatment room two bloody weeks later. I must learn to be more assertive. I tried telling him that he'd stepped well over my boundaries, but he just didn't listen.

Was so flustered I forgot to mention bioenergetics, which is ridiculous – especially for an actor – considering bioenergetics is so inextricably linked with body language, and what it reveals about the unconscious. It was all very easy to trash Wilhelm Reich out of hand, but without him the whole psychophysical school wouldn't have been born and Alexander Lowen, the father of bioenergetics wouldn't have got off the starting blocks. Robert's emotional problems are so obviously manifested in his physical make-up, that this really was a serious oversight on my part. I'm slipping.

What am I doing writing all this down? I mustn't let Robert take over so much.

That acupuncturist is obviously a bit insecure, because she took offence where none was intended. I mean, acupuncture only really took off in this country in the mid eighties, but now it seems I've made an enemy of her. And then I went and said she could use my equator analogy in her damn book. Damn!

Also, must try and find a good moment to explain reasonably to Florence that talking about my bowels to anyone and everyone who rings up could be very bad for work.

ROBERT'S DIARY
JULY 20TH 8.15 pm

I thought I'd worked it out, it made some sort of sense, but that all faded as the day wore on and Nige told me how complex everything was. I'm utterly confused now.

Whenever I try and explain stuff to Nige, it doesn't work. Come to think of it, even when I'm not trying to explain anything, he seems to block out virtually everything and plaster the airwaves with information. He does go on.

Mind you, maybe he's right, because he has got this almost heroic ability to rise above and just ignore things that ordinary people like me would find really, really difficult, humiliating even. I mean, when Anna said that thing about having a physiology degree, his face didn't register anything at all. He didn't bat an eyelid. He's just a fat old git really.

Anna. Just realised that I met Anna today, and I've spent the evening alone and haven't had one fantasy about her. Just a warm background feeling. With white pants.

Must remember to book a table at The Ivy so I can finally pay Nige back.

6

TEN THOUSAND POLAROIDS OF BREASTS

Nigel and Robert are standing in the crowded Bow Street Gallery for the opening of two Czech artists' new work. In the large, white-walled room, thirty or forty people, many sporting unusual hairstyles and unnecessary dark glasses are standing talking. Too many people are smoking.

Robert I just don't get it. I'm looking at a nine by five black canvas.

Nigel   It's not meant to be easy, and they're not just black. This man has spent four years laying magenta on magenta on magenta. Every artist should make you adjust your position. Jaroslav Sorska spent twenty-seven months in Bartolameska prison in Prague, in a cell down the corridor from Vaclav Havel, and tries in his work to unite the elements of alienation, isolation and liberation. This latest series of paintings is his expression of the brutality of human communication.

Robert It must be me. I can't see it, I stand here and it looks like a blackboard to me. You can interpret all this stuff, Nige. How d'you know all that?

Nigel   It's written up here on the wall.

Robert Oh God, well, he can't be that good at communication, can he? If he has to write all that bollocks to explain his work.

Nigel   He didn't. That man over there with the mauve poncho wrote it. He owns the gallery.

Robert What, the bloke with the ginger comb-over? I was surprised they let him in! Anyway, it's not that I'm completely deaf to all modern art. I really like the other one, the woman's work. I could understand that, those polaroids.

Nigel   Yes, I thought that Rita Nietvnova's work would appeal to you, Robert. Typical.

Robert No, it wasn't just that they're breasts. It's something about the way they're all laid out in rows. It's made me think about the narrow world that I live in. It was an almost involuntary reaction, it sparked something off in me I wasn't aware was there.

Nigel   Yes, but Robert, you can't deny that the use

of ten thousand breasts is bound to evince a fairly
primal reaction. Especially from someone like you. It's
a pretty obvious device. The breast is, after all, the first
part-object-relation in infant development.

Robert Where does it say that? Oh, sorry, I thought
you were reading something the rusty old git with the
poncho had written. Go on, object-relation.

Nigel Object-relations. Okay, in the first six weeks of
your life, Robert, you thought you were omnipotent. In
other words, the whole world was you, and you were all
there was in the world. When you moved your leg, the
world moved its leg, when you were hungry the world
was hungry. When you had the satisfaction of swallowing,
so did the world. Gradually you will have made the
awful realisation that not only was your mother's breast
a separate entity from you, a separate object to which
you must relate in order to survive, but that it had a
will of its own. It could, if it chose, go away and leave
you screaming and bawling, full of anxieties and feelings
of separateness. So, as well as the obvious feelings of
love and gratitude towards your mother and her breast,
you experienced anger and resentment against being so
dependent on them, for being 'other'.

Robert D'you think Rita Niet-viet-nova-whatever is into
all that? Is that why she took the polaroids?

Nigel No Robert, I shouldn't think so for a minute.
What I'm talking about, I suppose, is Melanie Klein and
the work of the so-called British school of psychoanalysis,

which I thought might interest you in the light of your quest. Or have you forgotten about therapy now that you're so busy flirting with my overqualified acupuncturist?

Robert I was quite moved by the other Rita Niet-thingy piece as well. What did you think of that? That wasn't breasts. I know it looks like three turds on a griddle, but I've never known a piece of art to smell. How d'you think she did that?

Nigel   Oh, it's crude heating elements buried in glazed Czech peat. I quite like it but it's very derivative of Hirst. It's actually quite interesting, Robert, that that's the other piece you picked out. Because Melanie Klein would have gone so far as to say that this infantile rage against the breast I was talking about, could have been so great that the baby fantasised smearing faeces over it.[11] Does that have any resonance with you?

A very attractive, severe and starkly dressed woman arrives by Nigel's side.

Florence I'm finding the whole exhibition phallocentric.

Nigel   But darling, one of the artists is a woman.

Florence I'm going to go now. I'll see you when I get back from Cuba.

Nigel   Oh, okay.

Florence leaves.

Robert Oh Nige, that's your Florence, she's really beautiful. I wouldn't have to have all my sad fantasies if I was with someone like that.

Nigel She remakes the bed before she gets into it. She brushes her teeth five times before lunch. She eats her peas one by one.

Robert I suppose she did look a bit, well, uptight. You ever thought about dumping her?

Nigel Not possible. You know, Robert, I don't know why I didn't think of this before, it's been staring me in the face. Kleinian analysis might be the very thing you're looking for. Your aggressive envy of me just now is something that a Kleinian would be only too prepared to tackle.

Robert I'm not envious of you. I think you're brilliant.

Nigel Hmmmm. A bit of projective identification. Because I've been helping you with your problem, in a sense nurturing you with my breast milk, you have very ambivalent feelings towards me of love and hate. You don't want to 'own' them, so you 'manipulate' me into 'inducing' them in you. If you can't have the breast, no one can.

Robert Calm down, Nige. It's only an exhibition. Now, tell me more about this Beverly Klein woman.

Nigel Melanie. It's just that I wanted you to

understand that given everything I know about you now, I really think to go and see a Kleinian would be the breast thing for you ... best thing, I mean. I must warn you though that a great deal of commitment is demanded of the patient. It's four to five times a week, Robert, and it concentrates very much on the first few non-verbal weeks of your life.

Robert Good, well I'm glad we've got that one sorted out, then. Are you feeling okay? D'you want me to get you a cup of tea or something?

The gallery owner approaches them holding the arm of a dark-haired woman in leather jeans.

Covelly Mr Planer, I'm Graham Covelly. So glad you could make it. Let me introduce you to Rita Nietvnova, she's been dying to meet you.

Nigel Well, hello. My goodness me. I've been admiring your work, I particularly like 'Three Warm Archetypes'. It stirred something inside me which I didn't know was there.

Rita You are Neil from *The Young Ones*? Where is your long hair? Can I have your autograph for my daughter?

Nigel signs the back of a leaflet for her.

Nigel No problem, Rita. Tell me, where d'you find the inspiration for your work?

Rita   From my dreams, from my experiences, from the shitty men in my life.

Nigel   I see, dreams and 'archetypes'. Fascinating. So the three brown, um, things, could in effect be a symbol, a Jungian symbol if you like, of a primitive and, um, instinctual, ah, unconscious . . . ness.

Nigel hands her the signed leaflet.

Nigel   I was filming in Praha last year. What area d'you live? The Stare Mesto? Hradcany?

Rita   New York.

She rejoins a group of serious-looking art lovers.

Nigel   What an amazing woman! Such presence. I mean . . . obviously I don't mean that in any kind of sexual way, but . . . fucking hell! She's so . . .

Robert   I like her work but I'm afraid as a person she falls into my seventy-percent rejects category. But it was pearls before swine, mate, pearls before swine. All that symbols and primitive instinctual stuff, that was brilliant. It was wasted on her. Is that Jungian? Why haven't you told me about Jung before? It sounds just the thing I need.

Nigel   Uh oh. And now I need the toilet.

Robert   Okay, I'll come with you. I'm bursting after all that orange juice.

They go downstairs. In the Gents Nigel enters a cubicle and locks the door. He makes a very loud coughing noise.

Robert So tell me about Jung, then.

Nigel You're still out there, are you?

Robert It's alright. I'll wait.

Nigel No don't, Robert. Really, I can . . .

There is an almighty blatt with thunderous undertones.

Robert Bloody hell, Nige. Was that you? You should see someone about that. You poor fucker.

Nigel There goes any tatter of dignity I may have possessed.

A large sigh is heard from the cubicle.

Nigel Okay, Jung. The reason I didn't tell you about Jung, Robert, is that I didn't feel it would be right for you at this delicate stage of your development. It was hard enough getting you to understand the basic Freudian concepts of the unconscious, but C. G. Jung, who was actually a favourite pupil of Freud's but fell from grace, took it one step further. Or, one could say, one step beyond.

Robert Madness.

Nigel You remember when we talked about the

unconscious in terms of the super ego and the id? Which interestingly enough is translated from the German 'das es', which literally means 'the it'. Well, Jung developed the idea that there were areas of the unconscious that are common to us all, almost as if there were parts of your soul which are autonomous or independent from you. He called these bits 'archetypes'. He said that they manifest themselves through common symbols which are shared by all cultures. For instance, a schizophrenic in Neasden might draw a picture of the sun as a wheel in exactly the same way as is described in an ancient Aztec text of which he could have had no prior knowledge.[12]

Robert Wow. Far out. So, Freud does your willy and Klein does your poo and Jung does your dreams, does he? I'd be well into a bit of Jung. I keep having this recurring one about Danielle and climbing through a very narrow wet tunnel.

Nigel Well, for a start, Freud was quite interested in poo himself. And dreams, of course. In fact it was he who first used the interpretation of dreams as a way into the unconscious. But there's a subtle difference between Freud's analysis of dreams and Jung's. You see, Freud would have seen your dream as a distorted representation of a hidden or repressed wish, whereas Jung would have seen it as an archetype seeking to make itself known.[13] Jung would have thought of a dream almost like a hieroglyph needing translation, not interpretation. So, a Jungian analyst would encourage you to imagine a way further into the dream scenario, instead of using it as a Freudian would, to help you decipher your own subliminal conflicts. To Jung, dreams point upwards and outwards whereas to Freud, dreams point inward and downward.

Nigel flushes the toilet and emerges from the cubicle.

Robert So Jung is the one for acid heads. God, this really takes me back. Herman Hesse, Quintessence, trippy Tibetan posters.

Nigel Well, actually, you're absolutely right, Robert. Because of course the square-within-a-circle-within-a-square-within-a-circle shape of the mandala which appears on so many Tibetan posters and sixties' album covers is in fact the ultimate universal symbol. Jung pointed out that the mandala appears in one form or another in almost all ancient and modern cultures. It's in architecture from ancient Greek to Richard Rogers. It's even on this toilet window here. Look.

They both study the mandala pattern on the art deco frosted glass window.

Robert Oh wow, yeah. Amazing.

Nigel Isn't it.

Robert This is it, Nige, this is the one for me. I don't want to do all that breasts and shit stuff. Projective identification sounded far too heavy for me, I want to be all spiritual and spacey. Jung's my man.

Nigel Not so fast, Robert. The reason I didn't mention all this earlier is that it seemed to me that you had a more urgent and pressing problem. A 'clear and present danger' if you wish.

Robert Well, you were quite happy for me to do five times a week for seventeen years with Beverly Klein.

Nigel Melanie! I was wrong! Can't I be wrong just this once? I was merely trying to test your resolve. After all I've done for you, the hours I've spent helping you, and I make one little mistake and the whole world crashes down on me! Anyway, embarking on a course of Jungian analysis is more a journey into enlightenment than a digging into the murky depths of your psyche. To tell you the truth, when you first rang me, I didn't think someone who scratches all night to get over a minor heartbreak would have the time and spiritual energy to attempt to make contact with something as universal and profound as the collective unconscious, to use Jung's phrase. Monosymptomatic phobias and mundane sexual disorders, as I told you weeks ago, are better and more swiftly treated by behaviourists, clinical psychologists and any number of other cognitive therapists. Jungian analysis is more of an education.

Robert No, but I've changed. I don't scratch any more, haven't for weeks, don't you see. You've helped me through these first few stages. Boy, do I owe you that lunch at The Ivy. I even spoke to Danielle the other night and it was okay, which actually was a bit of a relief. I never trusted her anyway, and now I think I was right not to. I really think I'm ready.

Nigel Yes, but I'm worried you're jumping the gun.

Of course I'm glad you've found these talks a comfort,
I'm flattered even, but I mean, the fucking collective
unconscious contains the great shared events of time! I
mean, Jung actually said that 'in the collective unconscious
of the individual, history prepares itself'.[14] I mean we're
not talking about pissing around on the internet like some
psychological cyber-jockey here. And anyway, I'm sure
you were wrong about Danielle. You wait upstairs, I just,
um, need to go again.

Nigel locks himself back in the cubicle.

NIGEL'S DIARY
JULY 27TH 5.45 am

I wonder if Robert meant to leave his bag with his diary in it at the gallery last night? I wonder what Freud would have said about that? Now I'm going to have to go through the hellish decision of whether to read the diary or not.

What am I talking about? I have read it. All. What's the point of lying in one's own aide-memoire? Only, of course, if you were going to leave it somewhere for all and sundry to peruse. So, I suppose I can take his 'fat git' reference with a pinch of salt.

But I don't think he understands me at all. On the other hand, why should he, in the state he's in? Although now I'm not sure he really needs help as much as he says he does. He seems perfectly lucid in his diary, just a bit of an arsehole.

Oh dear. It's almost as if I'm counter-transferring onto Robert. If only I could think of it more as an 'amplification', as a true Jungian would, rather than a dependency.

No, I know what I'll do. I'll type the address label and post the diary and bag to Robert from Bow Street, and he'll think the gallery sent it to him.

I won't photocopy it or anything like that.

7

ACHIEVING TANTRUM

Robert, clean-shaven with his hair combed, dressed for once in a suit, looks up at a large building on Lyndhurst Gardens, Hampstead. He walks up the steps and presses the bell to flat number four. Over the intercom a guarded voice says, 'Yes?' Robert looks cautiously around before pushing the front door open when the buzzer sounds. Once inside, he winds his way up the oak-panelled stairs to a large, imposing door which has a security chain on.

Robert Nige, it's me. Robert. I've got it!

Nigel's face appears at the crack in the door.

Robert I've got the table at The Ivy! It's today.

We've got three quarters of an hour to get there, and it's definitely on me this time. I've found all my credit cards. Look.

Robert holds up his credit cards at the crack in the door. Nigel eyes them suspiciously.

Nigel   Robert, this is not a good time. Florence is due back from Cuba any minute. I have to . . .

Robert   Wey hey! Who is she? Get her out quickly. I'll get her a cab, I've got my mobile working again. Nige, you old devil, while the cat's away, eh?

Nigel removes the security chain and opens the door to let Robert in. Robert follows Nigel down a long corridor.

Robert   Yes indeed, lead in the old pencil, eh, Nigeathon? Shaggeroony royale, you old bastard. I bet she's young too.

Nigel   Robert, it's not like that. I haven't got a woman here, I've got four hundred and seven books about psychotherapy which have to be put under the immersion tank in the attic immediately.

Robert   Why?

Nigel   Florence doesn't know about them. About our talks. She'll be here any minute. Her flight landed an hour ago.

Robert   You poor sad bastard. I didn't realise it was that bad between you. Won't she even let you read them in the bog?

Nigel   Look, it's one thing for you and I to have this shared interest. That doesn't mean we have to inflict it on other people, like Florence, who might have a completely different take on the zeitgeist.

Robert You mean she's in denial and she won't let you have any personal freedom within the confines of your relationship?

Nigel   It took me six months to recover from a burst eardrum when she hit me with a copy of Fairbairn's *Psychoanalytic Studies of the Personality*. Look, are you going to help me get these books under the tank or not?

Robert I'll help you, Nige. But are you sure you're doing the right thing here? I mean, wouldn't it be better to leave the books, come to The Ivy ... and just not be here when she gets back?

Nigel   Very amusing, Robert.

Robert picks up a stack of books from the sitting room while Nigel pulls down the folding ladder from the attic trapdoor.

Robert Nige, let her find the books and deal with her own displaced fantasies of omnipotence in her own way. She's coming back, all springy and bright, expecting you here, she comes in the door, flicks on the light, she finds the flat empty ... and whooom, she's got to face her own ...

They hear the key in the lock downstairs. The colour drains from Nigel's face.

Nigel   Omigod. It's her!

Robert   Is there a back way out, have you got a fire escape?

Nigel   Yes, but I can't do this. I can't just leave her to find these . . . and anyway I'm not dressed for The Ivy.

Robert   Come on!

Robert slides open the large sash window behind the television, and they clamber out, running down the metal stairs as quietly as they can.

Nigel   I really shouldn't be doing this. This is acting out. It's acting out.

Robert   Yiiiii ha!

Nigel   Please, this is a residential area.

As they descend they pass a window to a large back room. A man is kneeling in the centre of the room repeatedly beating a cushion with a baseball bat and sobbing. He is watched calmly by a smiling old man with a white beard, and wire frame spectacles.

Nigel   Don't stand and stare Robert.

They get to the bottom and run across the small back yard.

Robert We're going to have to climb over the dustbins, aren't we?

Robert vaults over the fence like an SAS regular.

Nigel You're fit to get up there.

Nigel tries an easier route.

Robert Bad luck! I'm glad I didn't stand on that bin-liner. What is that, fish pie?

Nigel This is not how I . . . intended . . . today to happen.

They walk down the street, Nigel occasionally shaking his badly stained trouser leg out to one side.

Robert What was that guy doing in there?

Nigel Oh, that was Andrew McRae, the 'therapist on the stairs.'

Robert Sounds like a Joe Orton play. What sort is he then?

Nigel You know I'm not entirely sure. Cognitive, I imagine.

Robert Oh, yeah. Cognitive. What bus do we get for the West End?

Nigel Rather like the behaviourists I told you about

in the lift, a cognitive therapist would try and help
you change your behaviour patterns by helping you to
examine your own conscious thought processes. They're
more interested in your cognition than your unconscious.

Robert   Oh right. Have you ever been to see him?

Nigel   No, well obviously it would be entirely
inappropriate living just above him.

Robert   Can't we get a tube from West Hampstead?

Nigel   Just now for instance, when you came to the
door, you assumed, didn't you, that because I wouldn't
let you in it must mean that I had a woman with me?
You've so convinced yourself that you're a failure with
women that you were willing to bend reality to fit in
with your fears. In other words, that everyone else, me
in this, instance, is more successful with women than
you. You filtered out the information in front of your
eyes and manipulated it to make it consistent with your
preordained belief system. And that's what a cognitive
therapist would help you to adjust; the way your
'information processing' is biased.

Robert   By the way, Danielle told me about you and her
in Sheffield. No, it's okay, mate, I really don't mind. It's all
in the past. I'd have done the same thing. Go on though,
it's interesting, that cognitive stuff.

Nigel   Well, that's a relief, one less thing to worry
about.

Robert Anyway, I thought all the pillow-bashing that guy was doing would be more of what you'd call a gestalt.

Nigel Oh, um yes. Very clever. But in a gestalt, Robert, he'd be role-playing earlier memories and experiences, enacting unconscious fantasies, wouldn't he? The pillow might represent his father or headmaster or something. In cognitive therapy he'd be dealing with an actual current problem. Like coping with your anger by practicing relaxed breathing excerises. That sort of thing.

Robert Either way, you've still got to pay someone to go into a room and hit their cushions.

Nigel No, Robert, you're missing a crucial difference. If, as I suspect, Andrew McRae is indeed practising cognitive therapy, then the explanation must be that the man we saw is actually a baseball player, who has a very real and current problem with pillows.

Robert Whatever you say, Nige. Oh look, there's the 119, does that go to the West End?

Nigel Yes, it does, but Robert, I don't go on public transport, it's a thing of mine. We'll have to get a cab.

Robert Oh of course, yeah. I didn't think. You still get recognised, don't you? No one will ever recognise me.

The bus pulls away and they wait for a cab.

Nigel There you go again. Overgeneralising. How

d'you know no one will ever recognise you? That was a classic cognitive distortion. You're always doing this, aren't you? Making some 'arbitrary inference', drawing conclusions without evidence, 'magnifying' or 'minimising' the significance of events, 'personalising' them. In other words, groundlessly relating them to yourself. Or focusing on one tiny out-of-context detail and 'selectively abstracting' it for your own self-deprecating ends.[15]

Robert God, you're right. So, I suppose what you're saying is that I'm not really a failure with women. In fact, I'm more like God's gift. You know, fantastically, pheromonally attractive to all women? Wey hey!

Nigel I think you're missing the point here, Robert. I'm talking about the way you process information. There are more than two ways of relating to women, you know. It's not a question of total success or total failure. McRae would help you get rid of this 'absolutistic dichotomous' thinking.

Nigel hails a cab, it doesn't stop.

Nigel What is it about the way I hail cabs? They always ignore me. All cab drivers are shit! They're either racist bastards or they don't know the bloody way.

Robert Maybe he was going home for lunch.

Nigel Yes, alright. What time's the table booked for? Maybe I could buy another pair of trousers in Covent Garden on the way. Mind you, I haven't got any money on me. Damn.

Robert I'll lend you the money. Fuck it, I'll buy you the trousers, Nige! After everything you've done for me.

Nigel Don't be ridiculous. You can't pay me money for what I've done, I was just trying to make sure you were on the right lines. Just trying to give you some guidance. And I mean, bloody hell, McRae's been there every day, right underneath me. Sometimes the things closest to you are the hardest to see, aren't they? McRae would set you a proper agenda at the beginning of each session and give you homework assignments, which would challenge your automatic, maladaptive thoughts. Robert, you could collaborate scientifically with him to test the realities of your negative assumptions about yourself.

Robert Maybe a fantasy of yours is that I should go and see this McRae bloke, bash a couple of cushions and then come up and see you for a cup of tea and tell you all about it, when Florence wasn't there. Be a sort of surrogate therapee for you. Taxi!

A taxi squeels to a halt. They jump inside.

Nigel That is absolute bollocks. The Ivy, please.

Robert Nigel, are you okay?

Nigel Of course I'm okay. Don't be stupid. Are you okay?

Robert I'm okay if you're okay.

Nigel   Well, that's okay then.

Robert   'Cos if you're not okay, I'm not okay either. You do know that.

Nigel   Look! I'm okay! You're okay! Can we just forget it!

Robert   Because sometimes I feel that you're not really living your life. It seems you've sort of already written the script, and, well, there isn't a part in it for you. Well, not the real you. I mean, you read all these books, but you . . .

Nigel   Look Robert, I learned from a very early age that if something's worth doing, it's worth doing thoroughly.

Robert   There you are, you see. You decided at an early age that your script was all about thoroughness, but what about the other bits of you? The playful bits?

Cabbie   He's right, you know. You have to be careful not to repress your inner child, Mr Planer.

Nigel   Well, thank you very much, I'll obviously bear in mind what you say next time I'm . . . heading for a crisis. But my friend and I, well we've been actually talking about this kind of stuff, for, God, for some weeks now. Call us mad, but, um, ha ha . . . we don't really mean it, we're just, you know, researching, um, for a play.

Cabbie   Oh yeah. I'll tell you what, you're a comedian, aren't you? You'll like this. You know that book you was talking about, *I'm OK You're OK?* Ever heard of the politically incorrect version? *I'm OK You're A Cunt!* Ha ha ha.

Robert splutters with helpless laughter.

Cabbie I've had him in the back of the cab, you know. That Eric Berne.

Nigel. Eric Berne. Yes, the founder of transactional analysis.

Cabbie No, but seriously, it's the bible, isn't it? That *I'm OK You're OK* book? The bible of transactional analysis.

Nigel ... sactional analysis, yes.

Cabbie Charming man, we talked for hours. Call me thick, but from what I can gather, it's like, everybody's got these three ways of reacting, right? Basically, there's your adult state, there's your parent state and there's your child state.[16]

Nigel Quite right, the ego states. Adult, parent, child.

Cabbie I may have got it wrong, but when you're in adult mode, you're pretty much adapted to current reality. When you're in child mode, it's like a relic of the way you were when you were a kid, and when you're in parent mode you're sort of repeating your parents' attitudes.

Robert That's the trouble with all this therapy, isn't it? It gives people an excuse to blame their parents for everything. Which is too easy. No parents actually set out to mess you up, do they?

Cabbie Yeah, I didn't mean so much your parents' actual attitudes, more what you, as a kid, imagined your parents done. Like what you took on board. I mean, you're still carrying all that round with you.

Nigel Yes, quite right, and Berne would say that dysfunctions appear in relationships when people's ego states don't correspond. Such as both halves of a marriage saying 'I need looking after'. In other words, in child ego state. Or indeed, both trying to control, hold down, manipulate and beat each other mercilessly into submission, stuck in their parent ego state.

Cabbie Yes, I noticed when you got in the cab, Mr Planer was like the child, and you, sir, were looking after him. Nah, don't listen to me, I'm just a Berkshire.

Nigel Robert, I was intending to discuss transactional analysis with you, but if we look at everything all at once, we'll get so muddled, and you won't be able to differentiate. That's the trouble these days, people just mash up all forms of psychodynamic treatment into one big sticky tangle of chaotic contortions. One bloody mess of intestinal agony.

Robert But Nige, despite these therapies all having different names, you must admit, there are an awful lot of similarities between them? And surely they do feed into each other quite a lot? Surely the transactionals and the cognitives must have heard of each other and, I bet you, most behaviourists will have read all that dream stuff by Jung. It's like saying a so-called alternative comedian has never heard of Benny Hill.

Nigel   Yes, well one would hope that any professional carer would be carrying around a whole portfolio of skills. Each one informing the other in a sort of bursting lucky dip of procedural possibilities. However, it would be a mistake to think that all sorts of therapy are interchangeable, like some sort of homogeneous red soup . . .

Robert   Yeah, but I mean, your show *The Young Ones*. Everyone thought that was terribly revolutionary and shocking at the time. Everyone thought it broke all the rules, but it was still half an hour long, had a two-act plot with a premise and a conclusion, and four regular characters with catch-phrases. Bit like *Dad's Army* really. And there's nothing wrong with that.

Nigel   We didn't start out with catch-phrases, Robert. It was the audience's reaction that created them.

Robert   And I mean, *Red Dwarf* wouldn't exist if it wasn't for a hundred years of classical science fiction writing.

Nigel   I think we're getting slightly off the point here.

Robert   Okay. Take that adult, parent, child thing.

Sounds remarkably similar to ego, super ego, id to me. So if my self-critical guilty-conscience bit is my super ego, and if that was in control I'd like, be in parent mode, wouldn't I?

Cabbie Excuse me for butting in, but there are those, and I'm not saying I count myself among their number, but there are those who would strongly contest your last notion, sir. Arthur Janov, for one. I had him in here once. Very nice man, very polite. Good tipper. But he couldn't accept that there was any point of view other than his own. Even the possibility of it. For him, it was your Primal Scream therapy, or nothing. I mean he actually said, 'If one theory is valid . . . then other approaches are invalid.'[17] I mean, you what?! Alright, so you can get in touch with your deeply buried fears that your mum and dad don't love you, by being locked into a hotel room and challenged and goaded until you break down into your actual primal scream. And it can be a catharsis, can't it? But that doesn't necessarily mean that anybody who doesn't want to do it like that is a cunt. There we are, gents. The Ivy, that'll be six pound forty.

Nigel and Robert climb out of the cab, Robert gets out his wallet.

Cabbie Oh, I've had 'em all in here, you know. Ronnie Laing . . . R. D. Very funny man. D. W. Winnicott, one of the nicest men you could hope to meet. Always remembered the kids, asked about the family. Tony Clare, Bob Skinner, Susie Orbach. Course, she's not actually qualified as far as The British Institute of Psychoanalysis is concerned, I can tell you that for nothing. But then, what do they fucking know? But I must say, I've never had the coup what my old dad had. You know who my old dad had in the back of his cab, Christmas Eve 1938? Only old Siggy. That's right, Mr Freud hisself. And you know what, and I'm not saying this is where he got the idea from, but my old dad, been a cabbie all his life, always had a box of tissues in the back of the cab. Like a courtesy thing. And Mr Freud thought that was a good idea, and that's why, to this day, you'll always find a box of tissues in any therapeutic situation. Thanks then, gents. Lovely talking to you. Cheer up, Mr Planer. Might never 'appen.

The taxi pulls away.

Nigel   What an awful man.

They enter The Ivy restaurant and are greeted in the entrance lobby by a woman with closely cropped hair.

Gina   Hello, Nigel. Haven't seen you for a while.

Nigel   Goodness, I didn't recognise you Gina, with your hair all cropped up the back and . . . Robert would like that, wouldn't you Robert? Gina's from Sardinia, you know. Where the tuna fish come from.

Gina   Ah, Mr Llewellyn, table for two, come this way.

They are shown into the main room of the restaurant, which is a large and well-lit space with leaded windows on three sides. At the crisp white tables, next to sparkling wine glasses, the luminaries of the British entertainment industry lunch.

Their buoyant laughter riffles through the aroma of beautifully cooked food. Robert and Nigel are rapidly spirited to their seats as swift, discreet waiters carrying large plates high above their heads whisk between the tables like silent hummingbirds. An Esther Rantzen here, a Gary Oldman there, and surely in the corner with neatly trimmed beard, that's George Michael? They arrive at a table next to Michael Grade, the controller of Channel Four television who is finishing his lunch with Lynda La Plante. Through the following conversation, Nigel's and Robert's eyes are often drawn away to some instantly recognisable constellation.

Robert Nige, I don't know how to put this ... but I've been thinking about it ... well, a lot, as you know ... and I don't want you to think that I don't appreciate all the effort and the support you've given me, but ... I've decided I really don't want to go into therapy of any kind just at the moment ... I mean, maybe one day, and it's brilliant to have all this knowledge now. But just for the meantime, I'm going to give it, like, a break ... to see how I go. I mean, thanks and everything ...

Nigel Keep your voice down, and don't talk about fucking therapy in here.

Robert What? Why not?

Nigel We cannot discuss any kind of therapeutic support system in a showbiz situation. And if you don't know that by now ...

Waiter Would you like to order drinks before your meal?

Robert No, I'm fine. You go ahead, Nige.

Nigel No, I'll just have a mineral water, or shall we order the wine now? Actually, I'll have a double vodka and fresh lime.

Robert What I'm saying Nige, I suppose, is that I'd rather navigate the squalls of life in my own battered vessel, than try to rebuild myself to someone else's specifications as an ocean liner.[18] If you know what I mean.

Nigel gives a subtle wave to Angus Deayton and Maureen Lipman as they leave.

Nigel No one is trying to force you into being an ocean liner, Robert. You know . . . 'yachting', to pick up on your nautical analogy, is more concerned with trying to help you realise your own expert status, so that you can fulfil your personal potential . . .

The drinks arrive.

Nigel . . . as a twenty-foot ketch, that is.

Robert Look, Nige. I know you read an enormous amount of books, and you obviously know what you're talking about. And, I mean, I know it's none of my business, and tell me to go hang, but what sort of, um, for want of a better word, 'boating' have you done? If you know what I mean?

Nigel Oh, they've squeezed the lime wrong. God,

this fucking place has gone downhill. And there's far too much ice.

Nigel starts to finger out ice cubes from his glass and slam them irritably into the ashtray.

Robert   Have you actually ever done any? At all?

Nigel   Any what? What are you talking about, Robert?

Robert   You know what I mean, Nige. You've been telling me what to do, and without meaning to sound ungrateful, look, I'm not sure that you do know what you're talking about. Because it seems to me that although you know all the right words, you haven't actually done any, have you? Nige? Any at all? All I want to know is have you ever done any form of . . . of 'sailing'? . . . Nige? 'Rowing'? 'Ocean cruising'? 'Canoeing'? . . . You haven't, have you?

Nigel   What on earth are you on about? Are you mad? You sit there in your slimy suit, all smiles, wheedling at me. Bringing me to this God-awful place where they don't even know how to make a vodka and fresh lime. You're just a mess, Robert, a bloody mess. A tangled, knotted, sick pile of . . . doggy do! Excuse me, I have to go!

Nigel lurches up and heads for the exit. Unfortunately he hits the swing doors and inadvertently enters the kitchens. There is an almighty crashing noise akin to that produced by a man colliding with a fridge followed by a repeated kicking sound.

Nigel re-emerges from the swing doors and walks determinedly back to his seat, breathing deeply.

Nigel   Sorry about that. I think I'll stay after all. Er, another large vodka over here, please.

Nigel notices a tiny speck of blood on his knuckle. He licks it off, and smiles across the room at Jimmy Nail.

Robert   Are you sure you're okay, Nige? We don't have to do this.

Nigel   It's okay, I'm fine. I'm fine. Let's order.

Robert   Take some deep breaths, Nige. Why don't you try pinching your finger and thumb together . . .

Nigel   Why would I want to do that, Robert? Eh? Now, d'you think the scallops will be too gingery?

Robert   . . . you know, accessing your physical anchor cues. You know. Think of something really calm, pinch your fingers together and you'll be okay.

Nigel   Robert, will you just leave it? I'm perfectly calm. Perfectly calm, perfectly calm. Where's that bloody drink? Oh, not important enough, are we? They gave Chris Tarrant his bloody meal before they even looked at us.

Robert   Rumble strips, Nige. Remember? Slow down.

Nigel   Ah, here it is. And let's hope it's not just a glass full of fucking ice this time.

A waiter delivers a fresh drink.

Robert I've been so selfish, haven't I? Just thinking about my own stupid problems, not seeing what kind of pressure you must have been under. I mean you've got the diarrhoea ...

Nigel I wonder what the kidneys are like?

Robert You've got Florence ... there's Danielle and all the guilt about Sheffield ... which actually you needn't feel Nige. Really. You've got these obsessions. I mean, four hundred and seven books about therapy is a lot. It's too many, Nige.

Nigel What the hell do you know? You're just a one-off rubberised android, with no penis. You're not even an actor, you're just a coat-hanger for a lump of prosthetic latex. They only employ you because the BBC can't afford an animatronic version!

Robert I didn't want to say it before, Nige. But I think you need help. Really.

Nigel suddenly dives across the table and grabs Robert by the throat. Robert's head bangs on a window-sill as they tumble sideways. Glasses fly and shatter, a chair slides across the floor, tripping up a waiter. People at nearby tables pull back in shock.

Nigel You fucking arsehole. You fucking arsehole, I'll kill you. Leave me alone! You never let me play football, just had to play with your bloody train set, on and on with the bloody trains! I'll smash you! Fuck you, fuck you, fuck you!

Robert Nige . . . Nige . . . it's me . . . Robert! I'm not your dad. I can't breathe.

Two of the larger waiters help Michael Grade separate Nigel and Robert. The waiters escort Nigel to the exit, leaving Robert to follow.

Michael Grade Are you alright? It's Robert Llewellyn, isn't it?

Robert Yes, sorry about that. Thanks for the help. He's fine, really. He's really an amazing person. Really.

Michael Grade Yeah, poor bastard. It's a terrible business we're in, isn't it? The way it chews them up and spits them out. Talking of which, how d'you fancy being chewed? It's thirteen episodes, you'd co-present with Joan Bakewell. Studio and location. Subject psychotherapy. If you want it, shake my hand now.

Robert pauses for a moment. Nigel screams from the exit.

Nigel   You're all a big pile of poo. I shit you! I shit the lot of you!

Robert shakes Michael Grade's hand. They leave together. As Nigel is held by the door, Michael Grade leans toward the receptionist discreetly.

Michael Grade I'll pay for Mr Planer's damage, Gina.

ROBERT'S DIARY
OCTOBER 13TH 10.30 pm (14k used 346 available)

Weird. Danielle forwarded me my old diary. Must have left it somewhere. Doesn't matter. I've loaded all data onto the Psion, so I binned it.

Danielle angry with me last week. Again. This time 'cos I work Sundays. Told her to fuck off if she doesn't like it, 'cos I'm doing all this for her. Ungrateful cow.

People don't understand.

Joanie Bakewell told me that when Freud went to America he actually said, 'I am bringing them the plague.'[19] Great quote.

Using it tomorrow. Might help American sales.

Danielle reckons the show is cheap crap. Okay, it's just a thirteen-parter on late night Channel Four, but I spoke to this BBC bloke the other day who says they might want me to take over the Danny Baker spot! Yeah!

What's that humming? That's the sound of Jonathan Ross spinning in his grave, man.

Fucking rash has come back with a vengeance. All up my back. Thighs are a nightmare. Doesn't matter, not so bad on my face, and anyway doesn't show thanks to Michelle the make-up girl. Reckon she fancies me. Must remember to hassle Kev from VTR for some more Temazepam. I mean, I have to sleep sometimes.

I'm sticking this clipping on my notice-board as a reminder.

Grumpy Nigel's Drop From Ivy League

Ex-*Young Ones* star, drippy hippie Nigel Planer had an argument with a fridge today at London's chi-chi media eatery, The Ivy. Lunching with a friend, he spilt his lentils, levitated over the table and tried to strangle a customer. Singer and self-defence expert, Lynsey De Paul, eating at a nearby table, wrestled Planer to the ground before anything more serious than egos were bruised. Onlooker Phil Collins said, 'Nigel has always been tense, but this was a real set-to, Lynsey certainly raised a cheer when she decked him!'

8

THE CALL BACK

Robert is busy in his front room, the table covered in schedules for the following day's studio shoot on the Channel Four therapy series. The laptop is open on the armchair, the mobile phone recharging in its cradle. The phone rings. Robert snatches it up automatically.

Robert ... 'llo.

Nigel Hello Robert, it's me, Nige.

Robert Oh, right, I thought you were my production manager. Hi Nige, what're you doing?

Nigel Well, I've got a new twenty-unit phone

card, and Dr Grisholme said she thought it would be appropriate to ring you now.

Robert Oh, of course, you're in that place, aren't you? What's it like?

Nigel Well . . . um, it's . . . how shall I put this? It's a very benign regime, and a beautiful old house, lovely environment. Really.

Robert Good-good-good. Food okay?

Nigel Well . . . um, it's . . . how shall I put this? There's a good choice, and lots of salad. But, you know . . . not exactly . . . You remember Florence? She's been down a few times and actually brought me some coconut rice which she actually cooked herself. Which is really nice of her. First time she's ever cooked.

Robert That's brilliant. Look, Nige. Really nice to hear from you, but I really am up against it. That's good, that Florence cooked you the coconut rice.

Nigel But actually, Robert, I was, er . . . one of the reasons I rang was actually to see what the, um, programme consultant situation was like on your series, I mean whether you needed any researchers or anything? Because I . . .

Robert Yeah-yeah-yeah. No-no-no, fantastic idea, Nige. I don't know what the position is, I mean I'm just the presenter, I don't have any real power over decisions. But I'll definitely ask. Okay?

Nigel No, but the thing is, Robert, since I've been in Tenterden, I've actually learned so much, and not necessarily just from the doctors and the art therapist. Half the time they don't actually know what they're talking about. No, what's so interesting is the other patients. I mean, I've been taking some notes and . . .

Robert I'd really like to see them Nige. Maybe I could come and visit you sometime. Let's see. God! Wednesday the fifteenth is my only day off 'till next July. Oh no! Shit-shit-shit. I've got to go and see . . . er . . . my mum then.

Nigel I'm feeling loads better now, you know. I've stopped reading, I haven't read a book since I've been here.

Robert Oh, well done, Nige. Brilliant, man.

Nigel Oh God, the pips are about to go. I just wanted to give you this one idea. A new title for your show. *Couch Bananas* . . . what d'you think? That's 'couch' as in couch potato, and of course the therapeutic couch, and 'bananas' as in completely out of your head. *Couch Bananas*. It's good, isn't it? . . . Robert? . . . oh.

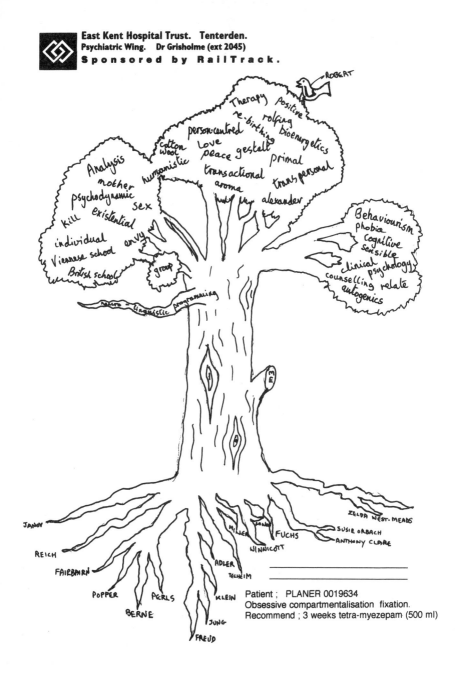

BLUFF YOUR WAY TO MENTAL HEALTH

While in principle the authors are thoroughly opposed to the stereotyping of any professional group, we feel that by categorising the various therapists into their necessarily brief character summaries, the individual patient/client/analysand may be empowered to match their own set of uniquenesses with the appropriate practitioner.

Freudian Analyst

An uptight anally-retentive Presbyterian, who lives in Hampstead because he wishes he was Jewish.
Distinguishing feature: Will always wear a lemon-yellow pullover.
Couch rating: ***** No eye contact.
Length of treatment: Why give up breakfast, analysis will become part of your life.

Kleinian Analyst

A profusely intelligent woman with a history of suspected spousal abuse.
Distinguishing feature: Looks alarmingly like Angelica Houston.
Couch rating: **** Occasional, but disturbing eye contact.
Length of treatment: Until therapist dies.

Jungian Analyst

Large male in loud waistcoat, cravat and Santa Claus beard.

Distinguishing feature: Hands you runic stone on first meeting.

Couch rating: **** Sits to the side, but you may catch glimpse of blinding waistcoat.

Length of treatment: Until the treatment transforms into a joint sculpture pilgrimage to Crete.

Adlerian Analyst, or, sorry, Therapist

Think John Alderton and you've got him.

Most likely to say: 'Well, we use a bit of everything here.'

Couch rating: ** Both chair and couch available.

Length of treatment: You'll be ready in another year. Maybe.

Cognitive Therapist

Neat-bodied Australian who would have photographs of his children on his desk if it were beneficial. Runs in marathons.

Distinguishing feature: Colour coded folders on spotless desk.

Couch rating: * Sit on chairs.

Length of treatment: Until he returns to Sydney.

Transactional Analyst

Person whose past experience has broadened their therapeutic skills and deepened their understanding of the human condition.

Distinguishing feature: Jailbird tattoo between thumb and forefinger which clashes with upper middle class accent.

Couch rating: * He/she sits in large armchair, you sit on hardbacked rattan stool.
Length of treatment: 1 month or until he/she is sent down again.

Person Centred Therapist
Mum.
Distinguishing feature: What does your mother mean to you?
Couch rating: 0. She's on the couch with you.
Length of treatment: You decide, dear.

Gestalt Therapist
Barrel-chested Canadian with braided beard. Will usually have built own tub-centred home in forest area.
Distinguishing feature: Difficult to see because he will stand well within your personal focus zone.
Couch rating: Use me as your couch.
Length of treatment: How much can you take?

Primal Therapist
Diminutive New Yorker with spittle problem.
Distinguishing feature: Stockinged feet. Leave shoes at door.
Couch rating: We threw the couch out of the fucking window man!
Length of treatment: In the padded room, time has no meaning.

Art Therapist
Very nice woman with HB pencil through loosely tied bun.
Distinguishing feature: Bible in smock pocket.

Couch Rating: The model lies on the couch, you stand at your easel.
Length of Treatment: Depends who wins the next election.

Occupational Therapist

Vocationally zealous nurse with a talent for carpentry.
Distinguishing feature: The nylon uniform.
Couch Rating: Finish your bi-plane first then we'll make a couch.
Length of Treatment: Until the tea trolley comes around.

Alexander Technique

Failed actress with nice neck.
Distinguishing feature: Sense of humour, despite special relaxed breathing.
Couch rating: 0. You lie on a table.
Length of treatment: Until you stop not standing up straight and have good use.

Aromatherapist/Reflexologist/Shiatsu/ Rolfing/Herbalist

Post cardiac advertising executive who has made a life choice.
Distinguishing feature: Impossibly clean.
Couch Rating: 0. Table again.
Length of Treatment: 45 minutes to an hour.

Clinical Psychologist

Hugely experienced lecturer in psychology who is given tiny room at back of major teaching hospital near laundry chute once a week, where she sees people who really do need help.

Distinguishing feature: Relaxed dress code, large stainless steel contemporary brooch.
Couch rating: 0. Plastic hospital chair.
Length of treatment: 3 or 4 sessions at most, or until department closed by Hospital Trust.

Couples Counsellors

A married couple who, like your parents, it's impossible to imagine having sex.
Distinguishing feature: Can say penis without flinching.
Couch rating: **** very good, except you have to sit next to your partner with whom you're finding it impossible to have sex.
Length of treatment: 3 or 4 sessions at most, I promise.

Psychiatrist

Dynamic Albert Finney with a goatee beard.
Distinguishing feature: Not overly sympathetic to any of the above.
Couch rating: You'll feel a little prick and then you'll be able to relax.
Length of treatment: Depends on the court.

REFERENCES

1 Miller, Alice, *The Untouched Key*, Virago, London, 1990

2 Innes (VFbb. eBD), Neil, *The Innes Book of Records*, BBC TV, London, 1990

3 Freud, S, & Breuer, J, *Studies in Hysteria*, Hogarth, London, 1985

4 O'Connor, J, & Seymour, J, *Introducing Neuro Linguistic Programming: Psychological Skills for Understanding and Influencing People*, Thorsons, London, 1990

5 O'Connor, J, & Seymour, J, *Introducing Neuro Linguistic Programming: Psychological Skills for Understanding and Influencing People*, Thorsons, London, 1990

6 Freud, Sigmund, *Analysis, Terminable and Interminable*, Hogarth, London, 1964

7 Sandler, Anne Marie, *Anna Freud Memorial Lecture*, Middlesex Hospital, 1993

8 Freud, Sigmund, *The Ego and the Id*, Hogarth, London, 1951

9 Rogers, Carl, *On Becoming a Person*, Houghton Mifflin, London, 1961

10 Kovel, Joel, *A Complete Guide to Therapy*, Pantheon Books, USA, 1976

11   Klein, Melanie, *The Psycho Analysis of Children*, Hogarth, London, 1932

12   Kovel, Joel, *A Complete Guide to Therapy*, Pantheon Books, USA, 1976

13   Jung, CG, *Man and his Symbols*, WH Allen, London, 1964

14   Jung, GC, *Analytical Psychology: It's Theory and Practice*, Routledge, London, 1968

15   Moorey, Sterling, 'Cognitive Therapy', *Individual Therapy* edited by Windy Dryden, Oxford University Press, Oxford, 1990

16   Sills, Charlotte, 'Transactional Analysis', *Therapists on Therapy* edited by Bob Mullen, Free Association Books, London, 1996

17   Janov, Arthur, *The Primal Scream*, Sphere, New York, 1973

18   Moorey, Sterling, 'Cognitive Therapy', *Individual Therapy* edited by Windy Dryden, Oxford University Press, Oxford, 1990

19   Kovel, Joel, *A Complete Guide to Therapy*, Pantheon Books, USA, 1976